MY FIRST
PIANO
Adventure®

FOR THE YOUNG BEGINNER
by Nancy and Randall Faber

Hello! I'm Tap, the music firefly.
Look for me throughout the book!

This book belongs to:

Progress Chart

Audio

Friends at the Piano

1. Can you name 3 or 4 of your friends?

2. Guess what? Now you have 6 more friends.
   Point to us and say our names with your teacher.

Katie

Carlos

Dallas

Marta
and
Millie
the twins

Mrs. Razzle-Dazzle
the piano teacher

FF1

Roll Call

Steady Beat

Tap a steady beat on your lap as you listen to the audio.
Enjoy learning the words and singing along!*

Sing

Friends at the piano, we're a band of friends!
Meet Millie, meet Marta, they're the twins.
Hey, Carlos. Hey, Dallas. Katie, too.
Mrs. Razzle-Dazzle is tapping with you.

**Chant and
tap the beat**

Tap the beat! Roll Call, please!

Millie 2 3 4 5 6 7 8,
Marta 2 3 4 5 6 7 8,
Carlos 2 3 4, Dallas 2 3 4,
Katie 2 3 4, Mrs. Raz-zle-Daz-zle,
Raz-zle, Raz-zle-Daz-zle.

Paste your
picture here.

**Drum roll
with hands**

Drum roll now for you, Yea!
Friends at the piano!

*Teacher Note: Students may take several weeks to learn the words and name of each "friend."

The "I'm Great" Pose

Posture at the Piano

Carlos

Millie

Marta

1. Sit **STRAIGHT** and **TALL** on the front part of the bench.

2. With arms straight, your knuckles should touch the **FALLBOARD**. If you have to lean, move the bench forward or backward.

Dallas

1 2 3 4 5 6 7 8 9 10 !

Katie

3. Silently place your hands in a loose fist on the **KEYS**. Your arms should be level with the keyboard. If not, you may need to sit on a cushion. Is your back still straight?

   This is your **I'M GREAT POSE!**

4. Try the I'm Great Trick!

   Balance a small stuffed animal on your head. Can you keep your great **POSTURE** while your teacher counts to 10?

Sounds on the Piano
Exploring the Keyboard

1. Play some **WHITE KEYS** all over the piano keyboard.

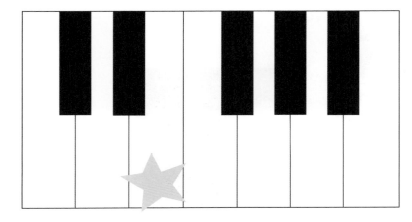

2. Find the **BLACK KEYS** and play some all over the piano keyboard.

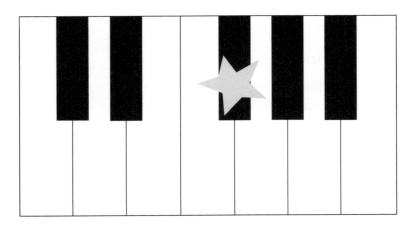

3. Find the **FALLBOARD** and create knocking sounds with loose fists. Then tap the **PIANO BENCH.**

Can you knock and chant your name?

4. Create some **SOFT** sounds anywhere on the keyboard.

5. Create some **LOUD** sounds anywhere on the keyboard.

6. Create some very **SHORT** sounds on the piano. Bounce your fingers quickly off the keys!

7. Create some very **LONG** sounds on the piano. Hold the keys down until the sound has completely faded away. Time it with a second-hand watch!

♩ Can you find Tap?

Will You Play?
Improvising with a Duet

soft | loud | long | short

1. Your teacher will play a musical question. Create the answer by making sounds together at the piano.

2. Circle a character at the bottom of the page each time you play this song. Can you find Tap?

Teacher Duet:

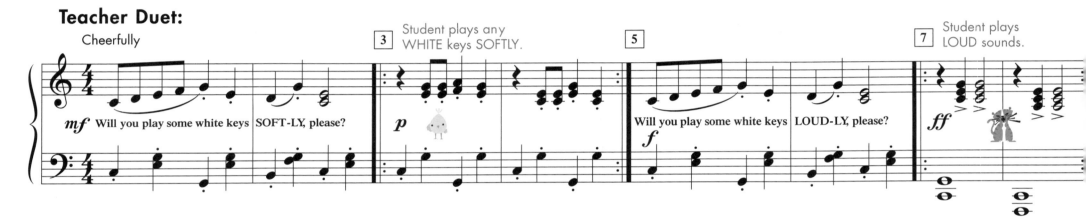

Cheerfully

3 Student plays any WHITE keys SOFTLY.

5

7 Student plays LOUD sounds.

mf Will you play some white keys SOFT-LY, please?

p

Will you play some white keys LOUD-LY, please?

ff

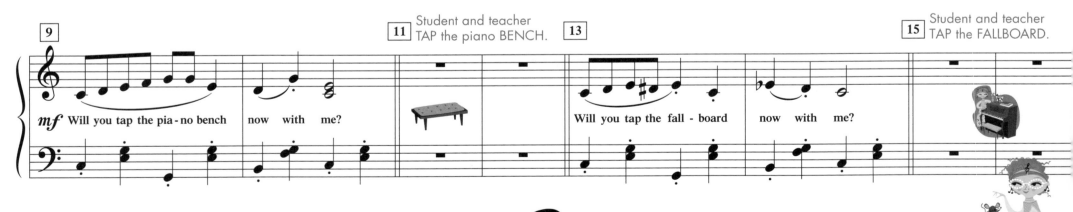

9

11 Student and teacher TAP the piano BENCH.

13

15 Student and teacher TAP the FALLBOARD.

mf Will you tap the pia-no bench now with me?

Will you tap the fall-board now with me?

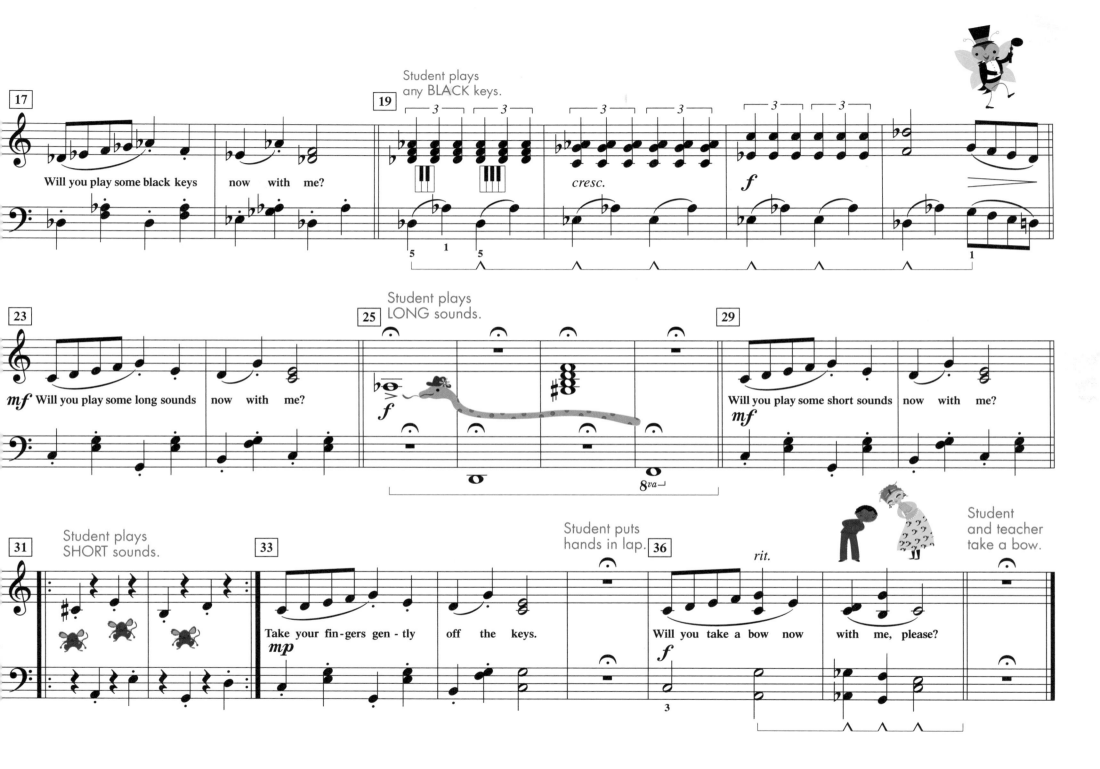

Stone on the Mountain

Technique: Arm Weight and Round Hand Shape

1. Pretend you have beautiful round stones in your hands. Katie's stone is red. What color is your stone?

2. Learn the words and do the motions for this song with your teacher. Can you chant with the voices on the audio?

3. Your teacher will demonstrate one of the pictures. Point to the one that matches. Then you be the teacher!

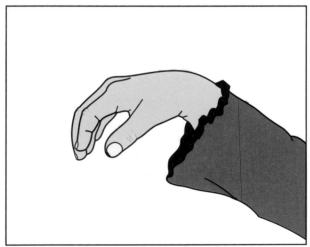

Stone on the mountain

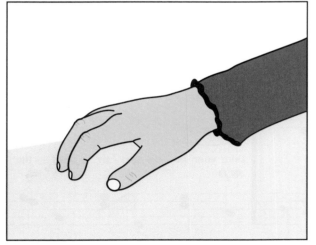

falls to the ground.
(Let the weight of your arm drop freely into your lap.)

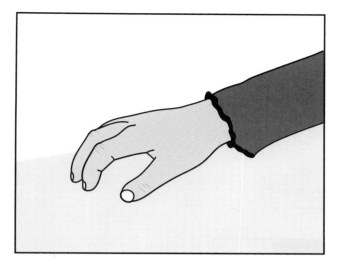

Hold it, mold it,

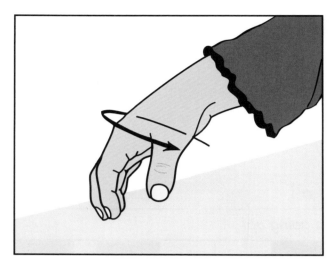

roll it around.

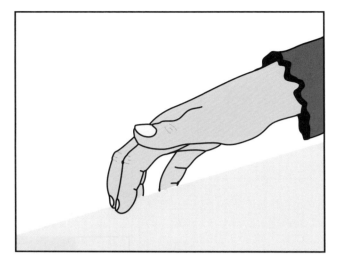

**Lift your thumb,
tap 1-2-3.**

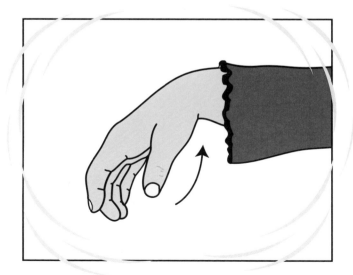

WHOOSH! goes the wind

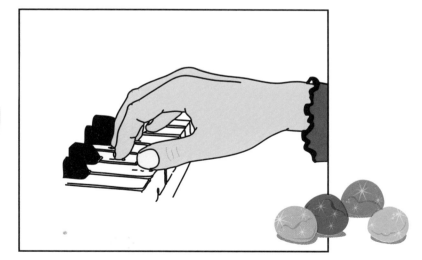

and land on the keys.

Check yourself: Are you still holding your stone?
Is your hand rounded, resting gently on the keys?

The Name Game

Middle Black Key Song

Demonstrate each step for the student:

1. With either hand, make an "O" shape with your thumb and pointer fingers.

2. Start on a MIDDLE group of 2-black-keys and play up and down, singing the words.

3. To end, chant and play your name on any black key.

"Let's   all   play   a   game."

Play and sing going up!

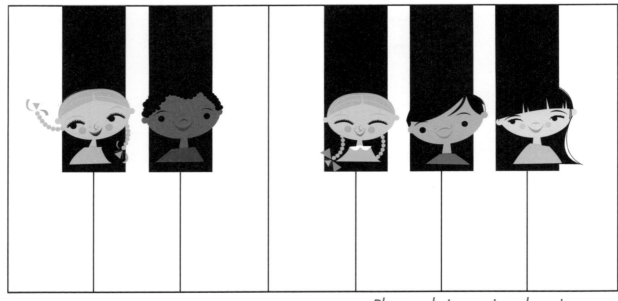

Play and sing going down!

"Play and say your name!"

For Teacher Use: (Play on the MIDDLE black keys. Use a braced finger 2 to demonstrate.)

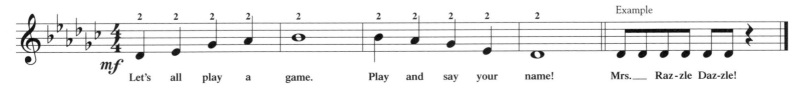

mf

Let's all play a game.   Play and say your name!   Mrs.___ Raz-zle Daz-zle!

Extra verses:
Let's all play a game.
Play your mother's name!
...father's name!
...grandma's name!
...doggie's name!

Demonstrate each step for the student:

1. Make an "O" shape with each hand as shown.

2. Your teacher will start on the LOWEST white key and play and chant *Tiger, Tiger*. Watch carefully!

3. Your turn to copy. Your teacher will guide you as you play and chant.

Tiger, Tiger
Low White Key Song

Lowest white keys!

Play and chant loudly:

Ti-ger, ti-ger, might-y roar.___

ROAR!

For Teacher Use: (Play on the LOWEST A-C keys to demonstrate.)

R.H.

L.H.

𝆑 Ti - ger,   ti - ger,   might - y   roar.   ROAR!

19

Left Hand and Right Hand
Exploring Finger Numbers

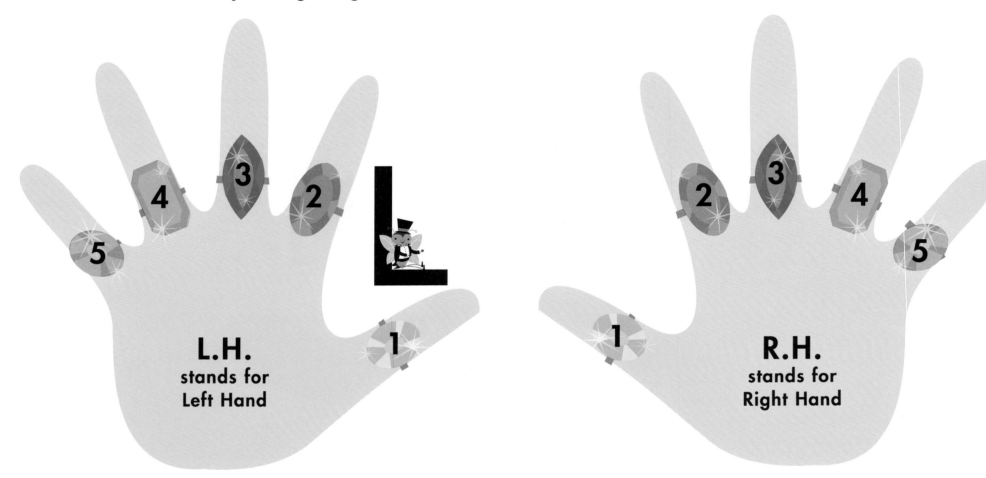

L.H.
stands for
Left Hand

R.H.
stands for
Right Hand

Tips from Tap:

1. Can you fit your hands over these hands? Can you find the **L** of the left hand?

2. Your teacher will sing, "*Mary had a little lamb, little lamb, little lamb. Mary had a little lamb, she pet it with her* **LEFT** *hand (or* **RIGHT***).*" Quickly put your hand over the one sung. Repeat!

3. Wave "hi" to Tap with fingers **1, 2, 3, 4,** and **5**.

4. Sing and do finger motions for *This Old Man* with the audio.

Teacher Note: Student may also use clay or a sponge for "dough."

1. Use a **round hand position** on a **tabletop**. Pretend you are pressing chocolate chips into cookie dough!

2. Learn the rhyme with your teacher and the audio. Gently tap the dough 4 times with each fingertip. Use **R.H.**, then **L.H.**

(5) # Cookie Dough

Technique: Firm Fingertips

Balance 1 on its side tip.
Press that little chocolate chip.

one, one, one, one

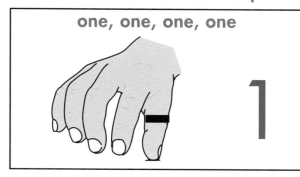

Balance 2 on fingertip.
Press that little chocolate chip.

two, two, two, two

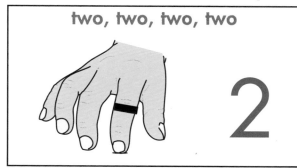

Balance 3 on fingertip.
Press that little chocolate chip.

three, three, three, three

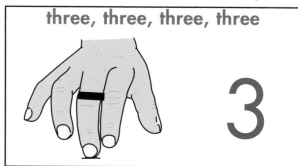

Balance 4 on fingertip.
Press that little chocolate chip.

four, four, four, four

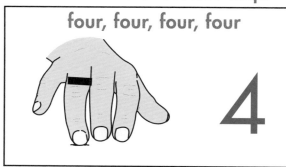

Balance 5 on fingertip.
Press that little chocolate chip.

five, five, five, five

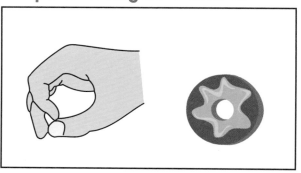

Make a round donut
shape with fingers 1 and 3.

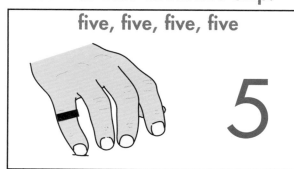

Teacher Note: Student will put thumb behind finger 3.

Dallas Dips L.H. Donuts
Sounds Going Lower on White Keys

When you play the low keys,
the sounds are lower!

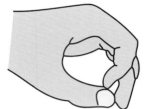

LOW ← **HIGH**

MIDDLE C

1. In the air with your teacher:

Pretend to dip a **L.H. 3-1 donut** in milk by dipping from your wrist. Say, "Dip, dip, dip, dip."

2. On the keyboard:

Start on MIDDLE C using a **L.H. 3-1 donut**. Play all the white keys going LOWER—to the left. Think, "Dip, dip, dip," etc. as you play.

3. Circle a donut each day you "dip your donuts" this week.

Dallas Dips R.H. Donuts
Sounds Going Higher on White Keys

When you play the high keys, the sounds are higher!

LOW ⸻⸻⸻⸻⸻⸻⸻⸻⟶ **HIGH**

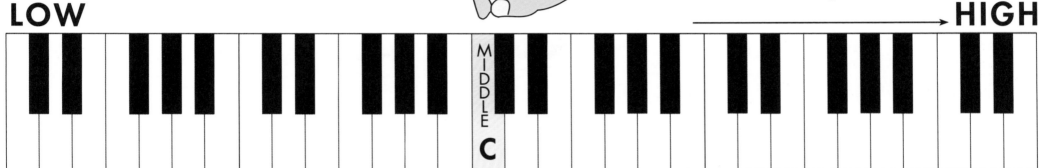

MIDDLE C

1. In the air with your teacher:

Pretend to dip a **R.H. 3-1 donut** in milk by dipping from your wrist. Say, "Dip, dip, dip, dip."

2. On the keyboard:

Start on MIDDLE C using a **R.H. 3-1 donut**. Play all the white keys going HIGHER—to the right. Then play, keeping a steady beat with the teacher duet or audio!

Teacher Duet: (Student begins on Middle C.)

✎ | WRITING BOOK 11 (A Jump Rope Story)

Twinkle, Twinkle Little Star

Tips from Millie and Marta:

1. First, sing and point to the stars on the page.

2. Next, rest your **R.H. 3-1 donut** on top of your teacher's hand as she/he plays the song using finger 3.

3. Now play with **R.H.**, then **L.H.** You may learn just the first page this week.

Repeated Notes

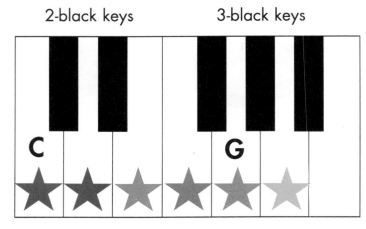

Note: A colorful paper wad, etc. may be placed on C and G to locate the first two pitches.

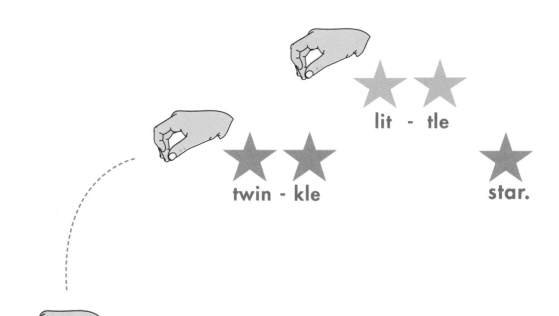

twin - kle

lit - tle

star.

Twin - kle,

How I

won - der

what you

are.

Teacher Duet: (Student plays in the MIDDLE of the keyboard.)

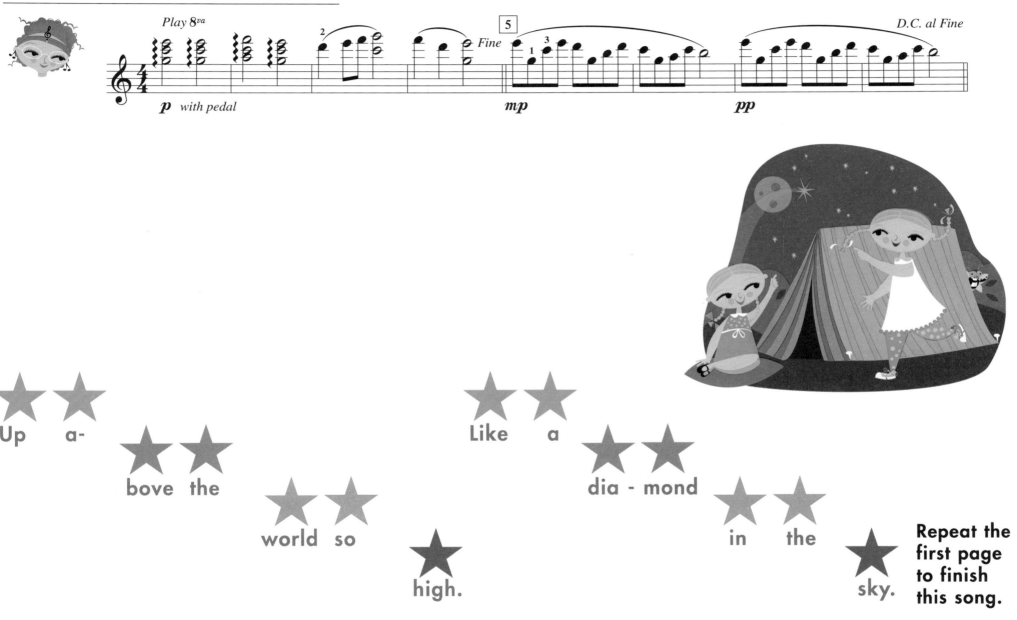

Up a-
bove the
world so
high.

Like a
dia - mond
in the
sky.

Repeat the
first page
to finish
this song.

4. Exercise your fingers with *What's in the Honey Pot?*
from the Writing Book, pp. 12–13.

Black-Key Groups
Two and Three Black Keys

Black keys are in groups of 2

and 3.

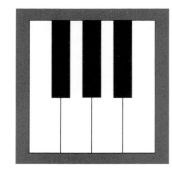

1. Play and count all the **2-black-key groups** on the piano. How many are there?

   Circle the friend with the correct number.

 **6**
Millie

7
Marta

 **8**
Dallas

2. Play and count all the **3-black-key groups** on the piano. How many are there?

   Circle the friend with the correct number.

 **6**
Mrs. Razzle-Dazzle

 **7**
Carlos

 **8**
Katie

FF1

Monster Bus Driver

Imitating Rhythms on Black Keys

1. On any  2-black-keys:

Imitate the horn sounds your teacher plays. Use L.H. or R.H. **fingers 2-3**.

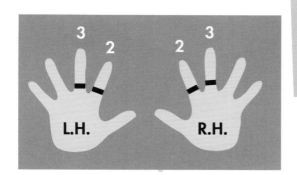

2. On any  3-black-keys:

Imitate the horn sounds your teacher plays. Use L.H. or R.H. **fingers 2-3-4**.

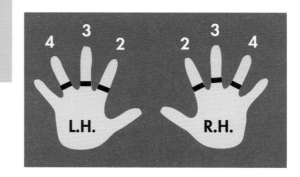

♩ Can you find Tap?

Teacher plays black-key rhythms for students to imitate. (Student plays 1 octave LOWER or HIGHER than the teacher.)

1a. 1b. 1c. 1d. 1e.

2a. 2b. 2c. 2d. 2e.

19

Wrist, Forearm, Fingertips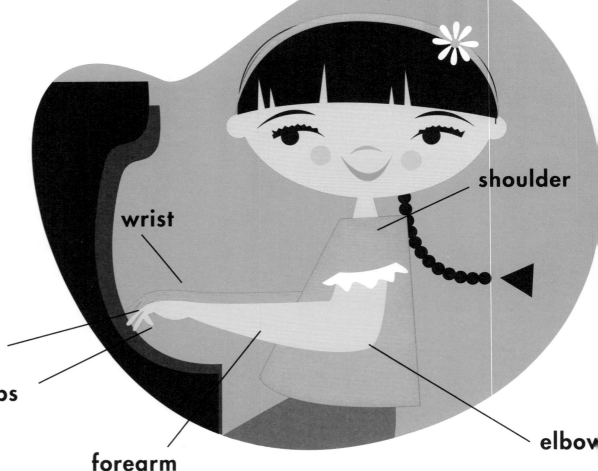

Technique: Introducing the Arm

1. Listen to your teacher sing the song (or use the audio).
   Point to the different parts of your body.

2. Play a steady beat on the **second to lowest white key**
   while your teacher plays the melody.
   Keep a great steady beat!

Wrist, forearm, fingertips—fingertips!
Wrist, forearm, fingertips,
I know how to find my
Knuckles, elbow, shoulder, too.
Wrist, forearm, fingertips—fingertips!

shoulder

wrist

knuckles

fingertips

elbow

forearm

Teacher melody for *Wrist, Forearm, Fingertips:*

Wrist, fore-arm, fin-ger-tips, fin-ger-tips.   Wrist, fore-arm, fin-ger-tips,   I know how to find my knuck-les, el - bow, shoul - der, too.   Wrist, fore-arm, fin-ger-tips, fin-ger-tips!

⑪ Mitsy's Cat Back

Technique: Flexible Wrist

Teacher Note: These wrist motions serve as preparation for the rainbow wrist gestures shown on the next pages.

1. Mrs. Razzle-Dazzle has a cat named Mitsy.
   Arch your **R.H.** wrist like Mitsy the cat arches her back.
   Repeat with **L.H.**

2. On the **closed piano lid**, do the motions for this song with your teacher. Can you sing with the audio?

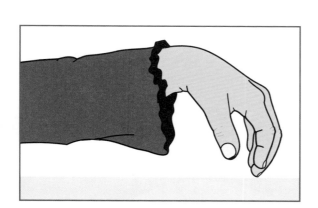

Do a cat back, do a cat back,

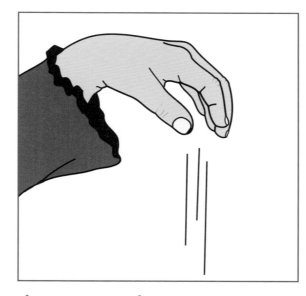

do a LEAP and

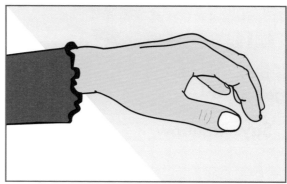

land upon your fingertips!
(Repeat all motions as the melody continues.)

Teacher melody for *Mitsy's Cat Back:*

19

Tips from Mitsy:

1. Point to each box where **L.H. fingers 2-3** play together.

2. Listen and watch your teacher play.

3. Your turn! Play and make L.H. rainbows to each LOWER **2-black-key group**. Your teacher may press the pedal as you play.

L.H. Rainbows

Technique: Graceful Wrist Motion

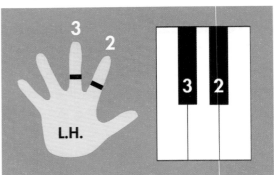

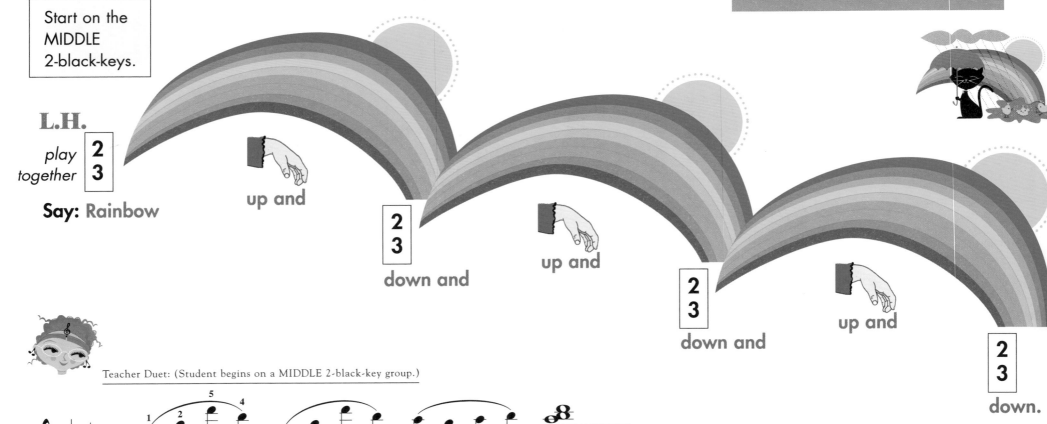

Start on the MIDDLE 2-black-keys.

L.H.

play together | 2 | 3

Say: Rainbow

up and

| 2 | 3 |

down and

up and

| 2 | 3 |

down and

up and

| 2 | 3 |

down.

Teacher Duet: (Student begins on a MIDDLE 2-black-key group.)

Chant: *Rain - bow   up   and   down   and   up   and   down   and   up   and   down.*

FF

R.H. Rainbows

13

Technique: Graceful Wrist Motion

Tips from Tap:

1. Point to each box where **R.H. fingers 2-3** play together.

2. Listen and watch your teacher play.

3. Your turn! Play and make R.H. rainbows to each HIGHER **2-black-key group**. Your teacher may press the pedal as you play.

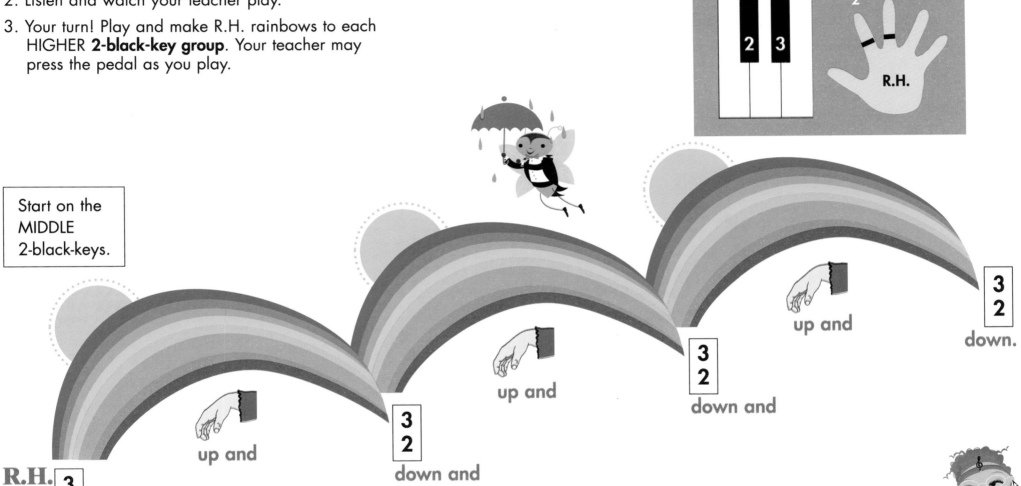

Start on the MIDDLE 2-black-keys.

R.H.
play together

3
2

Rainbow

3
2

up and

3
2

down and

3
2

up and

3
2

down and

3
2

up and

3
2

down.

Teacher Duet: (Student begins on a MIDDLE 2-black-key group.)

Kangaroo Show

Playing L.H. Fingers 2-3

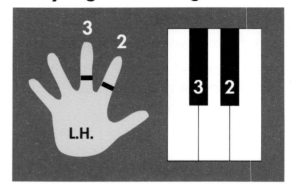

Tips from the Kangaroo:

1. Be the teacher! With L.H. finger 2, point to the numbers and say, **"2-2-2, together,"** etc.

2. Listen and watch your teacher play.

3. Your turn! Play and make kangaroo leaps to each LOWER **2-black-key group.**

> Start on the MIDDLE 2-black-keys.

play together

L.H. 2 2 2 | 2 / 3 |

Kan-ga-roo show,

BOING!

> Move DOWN to next *lower* group.

2 2 2 | 2 / 3 |

look at them go!

BOING!

2 2 2 | 2 / 3 |

Hop-ping so low,

BOING!

| 2 / 3 |

BOING!

Katie Scores!

Playing R.H. Fingers 2-3

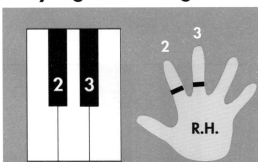

Tips from Katie:

1. Be the teacher! With R.H. finger 2, point to the numbers and say, **"2-2-2, together,"** etc.

2. Listen and watch your teacher play.

3. Your turn! Play and make the soccer ball fly to each HIGHER **2-black-key group**.

3
2

YEA!

2   2   2 | 3 / 2 |

we scored a goal,

Move UP to next higher group.

2   2   2 | 3 / 2 |

kick it so high;

Start on the MIDDLE 2-black-keys.

play together

R.H. 2   2   2 | 3 / 2 |

Soc-cer ball fly,

Tigers at My Door

Forte and Piano with Scale Steps

16

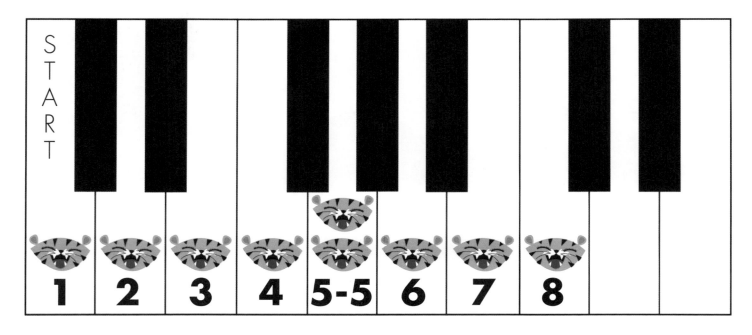

Teacher Note: A colorful paper wad, etc. may locate the opening C key. Two items may mark the G key.

1 2 3 4 5-5 6 7 8

f *(forte)* means
LOUD

p *(piano)* means
SOFT

Tips from the Tigers:

1. Circle f or p for the animal sounds on the next page.

2. Use a 2-1 donut and play the TIGER KEYS on the piano with the Teacher Duet or audio. Your teacher will guide you. Notice that "key 5" is played TWO times!

3. Listen for f and p sounds.

FF

TIGERS!

1, 2, 3, 4, 5
tigers
at my door!

5, 6, 7, 8
"Hey, let's roar and
stay up late."

f or p

RABBITS!

1, 2, 3, 4, 5
rabbits
at my door!

5, 6, 7, 8
"Hey, let's hop and
stay up late."

f or p

PUPPIES!

1, 2, 3, 4, 5
puppies
at my door!

5, 6, 7, 8
"Hey, let's bark and
stay up late."

f or p

SPIDERS!

1, 2, 3, 4, 5
spiders
at my door!

5, 6, 7, 8
"Hey, let's sleep.
It's getting late."

f or p

Teacher Duet: Repeat for "PUPPIES" and "SPIDERS" verse. Student plays 2 OCTAVES HIGHER.

f 1, 2, 3, 4, 5 ti - gers at my door! 5, 6, 7, 8 "Hey, let's roar and stay up late."
p 1, 2, 3, 4, 5 rab - bits at my door! 5, 6, 7, 8 "Hey, let's hop and stay up late."

19

Wendy the Whale

17

Playing L.H. Fingers 2-3-4

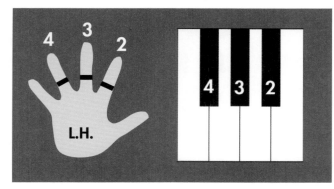

Note: The teacher may pedal
as the student plays.

Start on a
MIDDLE
3-black-key group.

play together

L.H. **2**   **2**   **2** | **2** / **3** / **4** |

f

Wen - dy   the   whale

Move DOWN to
next lower group.

2   **2**   **2** | **2** / **3** / **4** |

moves her   big   tail

2   **2**   **2** | **2** / **3** / **4** |

deep, down, and   low.

FF

Tips from Dallas: (pp. 32–33)

1. Be the teacher! With L.H. finger 2, point to the numbers and say, **"2-2-2, together,"** etc.

2. Listen and watch your teacher play.

3. Your turn! Pretend your hand is a whale, doing a slow leap and dive into each LOWER **3-black-key group.**

Deep Sea Game:

Turn off the lights and play this piece. Decide to play *forte* or *piano*.

Stay on the LOWEST 3-black-key group.

L.H. 2   2   2

3   3   3

4

Hold and listen!

Wen - dy   the   whale moves her   tail.

Double bar line means the end of the piece. (thin line, thick line)

✏️ | WRITING BOOK **20** (L.H. Twin Sounds)

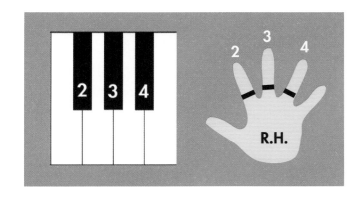

Playing R.H. Fingers 2-3-4

Tips from Millie and Marta:

1. Listen and watch your teacher play.

2. Your turn! Play and make a rainbow motion as you lift to each HIGHER **3-black-key group.**

Note: The teacher may pedal as the student plays.

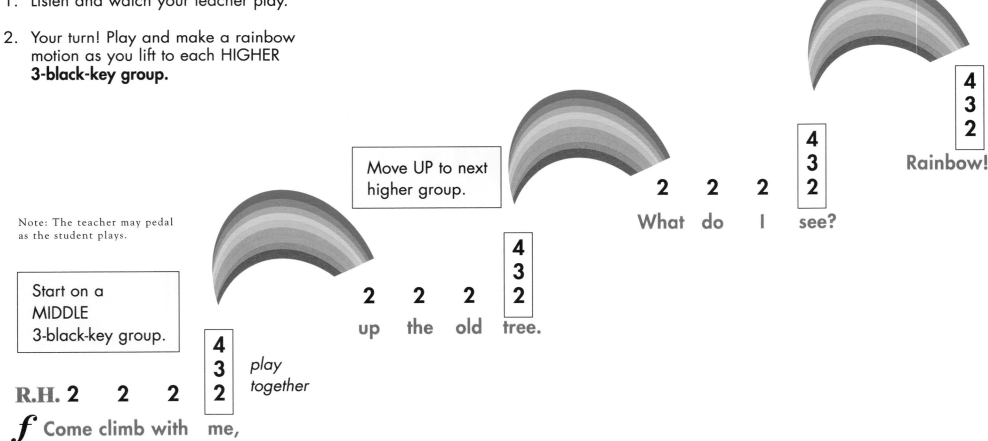

Start on a MIDDLE 3-black-key group.

Move UP to next higher group.

Rainbow!

R.H. **2**   **2**   **2** | **4** **3** **2** | *play together*

f Come climb with   me,

2   **2**   **2** | **4** **3** **2** |

up   the   old   tree.

2   **2**   **2** | **4** **3** **2** |

What   do   I   see?

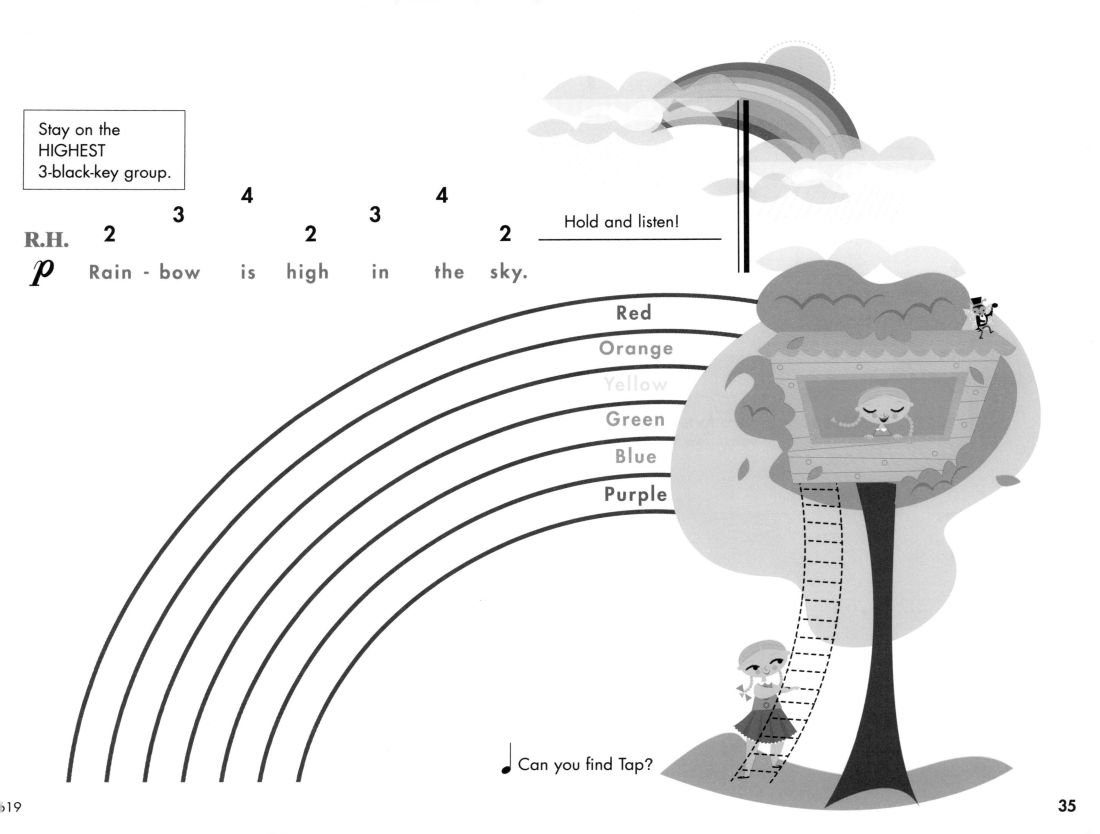

Stay on the
HIGHEST
3-black-key group.

Hold and listen!

R.H.

2   3   4   2   3   4   2

p   Rain - bow   is   high   in   the   sky.

Red

Orange

Yellow

Green

Blue

Purple

Can you find Tap?

Quarter Note = 1 Beat

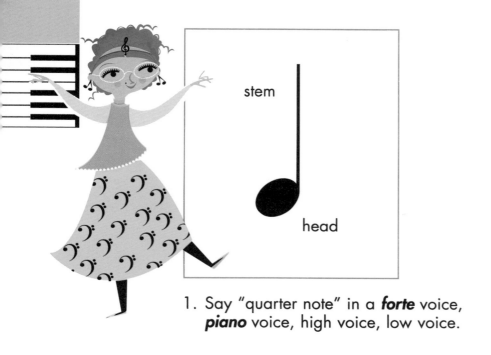

stem

head

1. Say "quarter note" in a **forte** voice, **piano** voice, high voice, low voice.

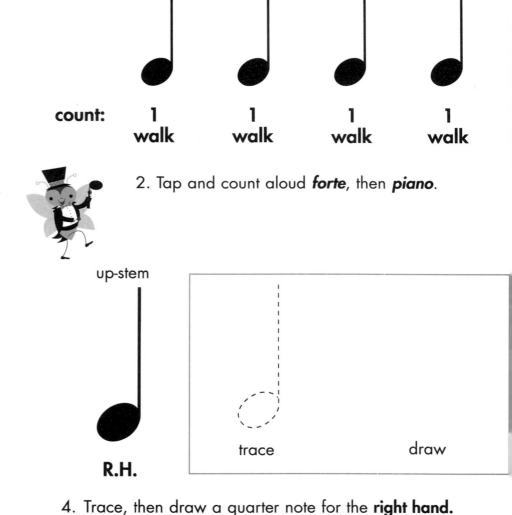

count:

1	1	1	1
walk	**walk**	**walk**	**walk**

2. Tap and count aloud **forte**, then **piano**.

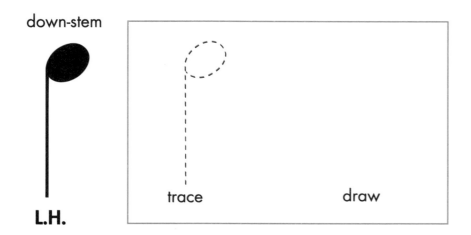

down-stem

L.H.

trace   draw

3. Trace, then draw a quarter note for the **left hand.**

up-stem

R.H.

trace   draw

4. Trace, then draw a quarter note for the **right hand.**

Dancing Feet
Tracking the Beat

Tips from your friends:

1. Circle each group of **R.H.** notes in **RED**.
   Circle each group of **L.H.** notes in **BLUE**.

2. Play each group with the correct hand on any key. Use a **2-1 donut**.

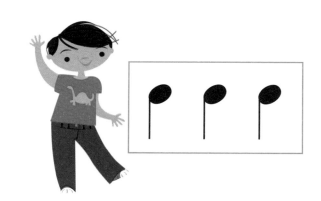

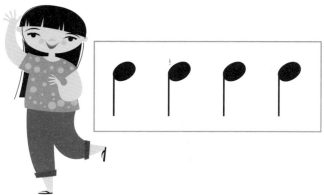

Keep a steady beat!

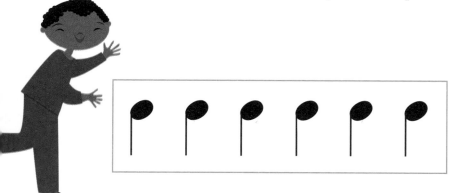

3. Your teacher will play a group of notes with the **left** or **right** hand. Point to the group you hear.

4. Have fun singing and tapping ♩ notes to *Buckle My Shoe*, Writing Book, pp. 22–23. **19**

20 Cuckoo Clock

Alternating Right and Left Hand

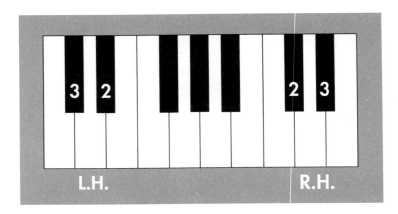

L.H.　　　　　R.H.

Tips from Tap:

1. With your teacher, tap on the door, floor, and the closed piano lid, saying,

   right - right - left - left, right - left - right - left.

2. Play on the 2-black keys and say, "right - right," etc. Is your clock keeping a steady beat?

Play fingers 2 and 3 at the same time.

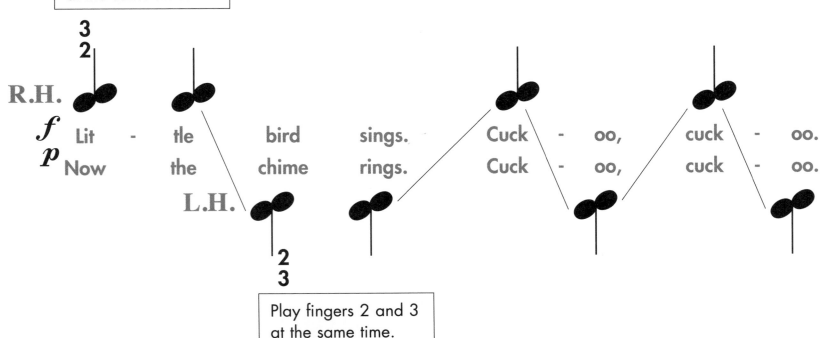

R.H.

f Lit - tle bird sings. Cuck - oo, cuck - oo.

p Now the chime rings. Cuck - oo, cuck - oo.

L.H.

Play fingers 2 and 3 at the same time.

Repeat Sign
These dots mean to play this page once again.

Teacher Duet: (Student plays in the MIDDLE of the keyboard.)

Student continues by "chiming" the time.
Teacher may depress the pedal for chimes.

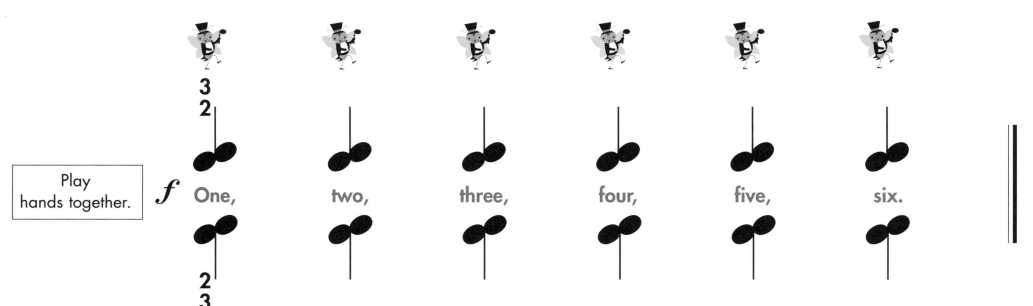

Play hands together.

𝆑 One, two, three, four, five, six.

The Cuckoo's Secret:
Decide a number that the cuckoo will chirp: **"2 o'clock, 4 o'clock,"** etc.
Play the first page, then chime the hour you chose on the 2-black keys. Your teacher must guess the time!

Dinosaur Music Night

Quarter-Note Song on Lowest Black Keys

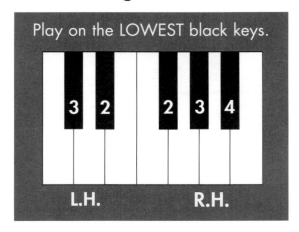

Play on the LOWEST black keys.

3 2   2 3 4

L.H.   R.H.

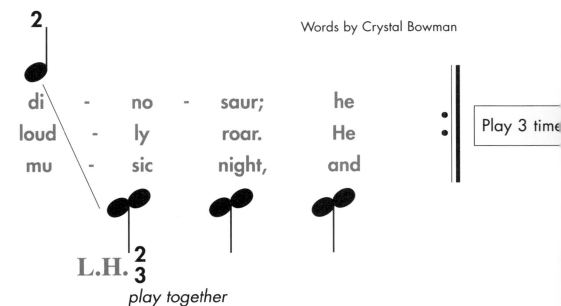

Words by Crystal Bowman

R.H.

4   4   3   3   2

f

This	is	my	pet	di	-	no	-	saur;	he
loves	to	stomp	and	loud	-	ly		roar.	He
came	to	my	school's	mu	-	sic		night,	and

L.H. 2 3

play together

Play 3 times

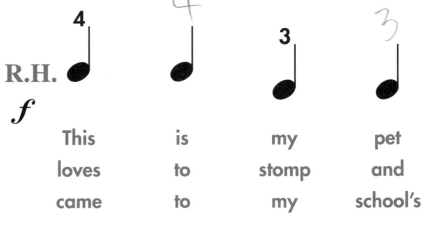

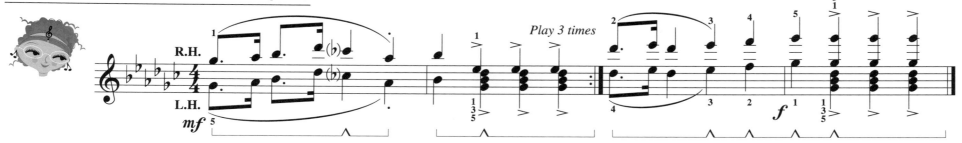

Tips from Katie: (pp. 40–41)

1. Can you believe who Katie brought to music night? Point to the notes as your teacher plays the song.

2. Circle the **repeated notes.**

3. Play **forte** on the LOWEST black-key groups.

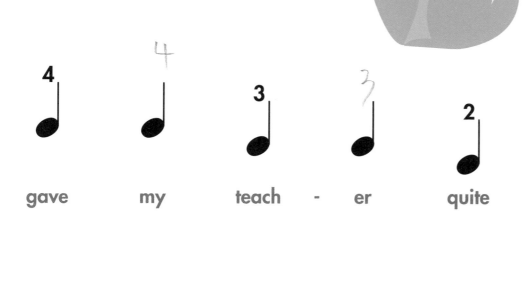

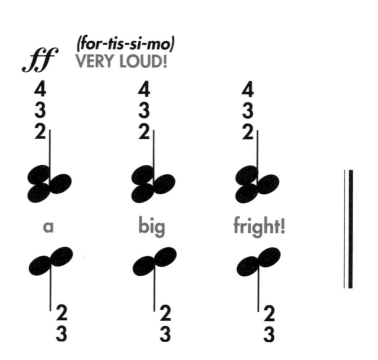

ff (for-tis-si-mo) VERY LOUD!

gave　my　teach　–　er　quite　a　big　fright!

Paw Prints
Blocking Keys C-D-E

the 3-white keys just below
the 2-black keys

For Left Hand

1. Begin in the MIDDLE of the piano.

2. To play a L.H. paw print, bring **fingertips 4-3-2** together. Play **C-D-E** keys at the same time.

2
3
4

3. Make a rainbow and play a "paw print" on each LOWER C-D-E group going down the keyboard.

For Right Hand

1. Begin in the MIDDLE of the piano.

2. To play a R.H. paw print, bring **fingertips 2-3-4** together. Play **C-D-E** keys at the same time.

4
3
2

3. Make a rainbow and play a "paw print" on each HIGHER C-D-E group going up the keyboard.

Wabbit the Rabbit
Finding C-D-E Keys

Dallas has lost his rabbit named Wabbit.

1. Your teacher will say the rhyme and point to a keyboard.

2. Play and name the key where Wabbit has landed.

Alaka ZOOM, Alaka ZAM! Wabbit is lost! Where did he land?

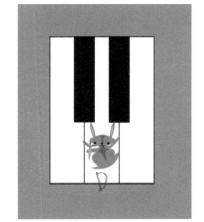

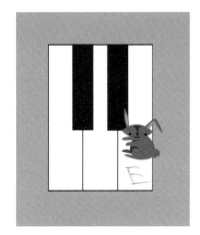

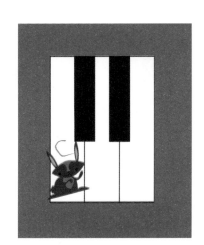

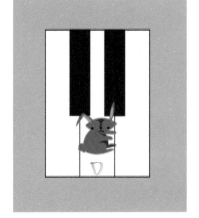

Little Lost Kitty

Quarter-Note Song on C-D-E

Tips from Millie and Marta:

1. Point to each note, counting "1, 1, 1, 1."
Use **L.H.** for *down*-stems and **R.H.** for *up*-stems.

2. Guide your teacher! Point to each note and say the **finger number** as your teacher plays.

3. Circle all the **repeated notes**.

4. Play on the piano, singing the finger numbers. Can you see your "stone"? (See p. 12)

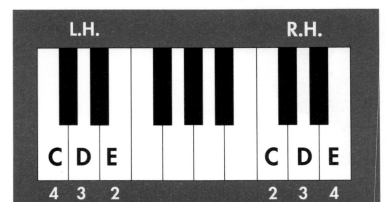

Words by Crystal Bowman

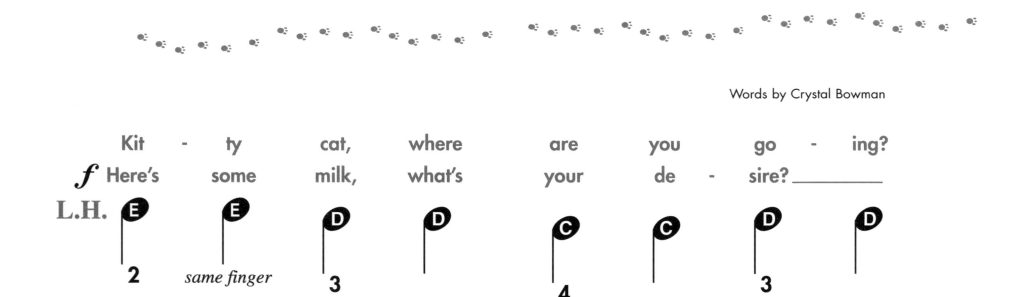

	Kit	-	ty	cat,	where		are	you	go	-	ing?
f	Here's		some	milk,	what's		your	de	-	sire?	_____

L.H.

E   E   D   D   C   C   D   D

2   *same finger*   3   4   3

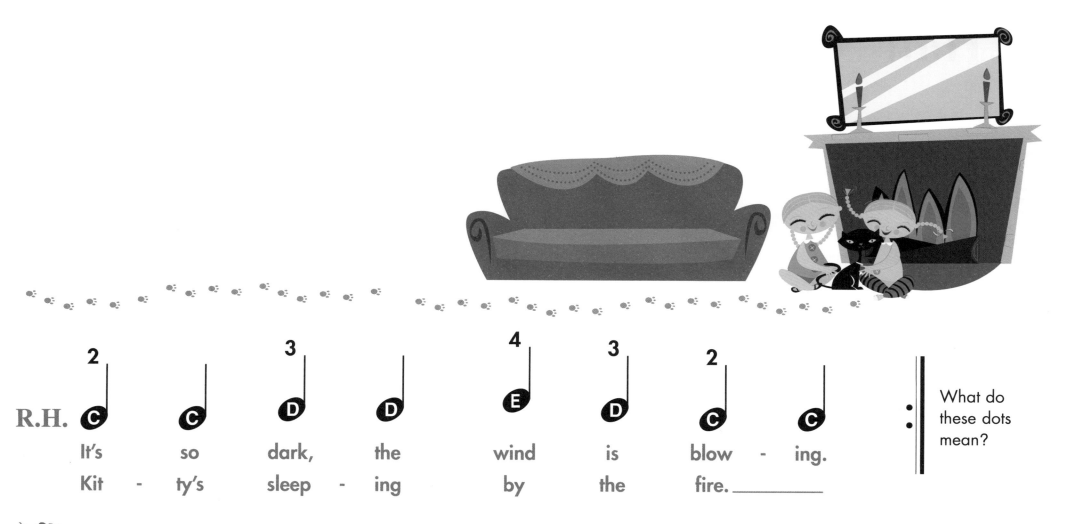

R.H.

2 **C** — **C** | 3 **D** — **D** | 4 **E** | 3 **D** | 2 **C** — **C** ‖:

It's so dark, the wind is blow - ing.
Kit - ty's sleep - ing by the fire._____

What do these dots mean?

Teacher Duet: (Student plays in the MIDDLE of the piano.)

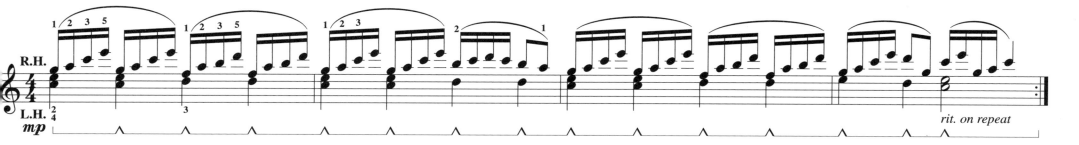

rit. on repeat

19

Half Note = 2 Beats

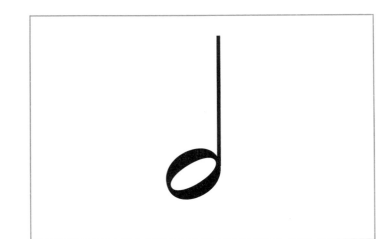

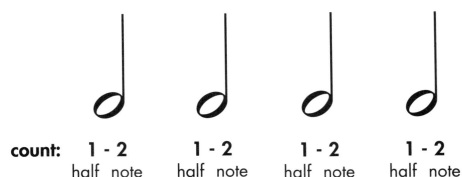

count: **1 - 2** **1 - 2** **1 - 2** **1 - 2**
half note   half note   half note   half note

1. Say "half note" in a **forte** voice, **piano** voice, high voice, low voice.

2. Tap and count aloud **forte**, then **piano**. Hold each note for 2 beats.

down-stem

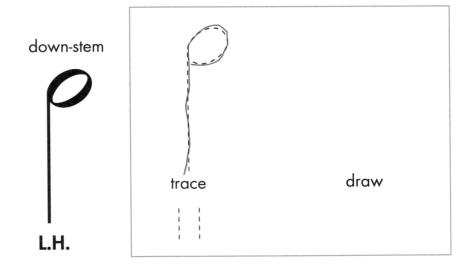

trace   draw

L.H.

up-stem

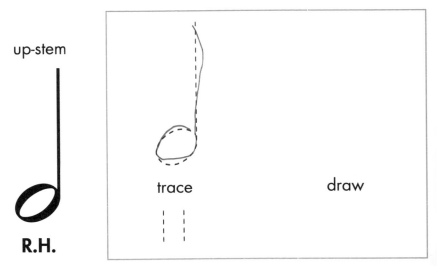

trace   draw

R.H.

3. Trace, then draw a half note for the **left hand**. Draw TWO slashes below to show **2 beats**.

4. Trace, then draw a half note for the **right hand**. Draw TWO slashes below to show **2 beats**.

FF

Band Practice!

Tracking the Beat

1. Circle each R.H. rhythm in **RED**.
   Circle each L.H. rhythm in **BLUE**.

2. Play with the correct hand on **any key** using a **2-1 donut**.

Keep a steady beat!

3. Your teacher will play a group of notes with the **left** or **right** hand.
   Point to the group you hear.

4. Have fun tapping ♩ and ♩ notes to *Turkey Talk* in your
   Writing Book, pp. 30–31.

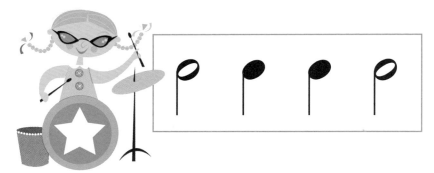

23

Monsieur Mouse

C-D-E Melody with Half Notes

Tips from Monsieur Mouse:

1. Point to the notes, counting, "1, 1, 1-2."
   Use **L.H.** for *down*-stems and **R.H.** for *up*-stems.

2. Your teacher will help you circle every group of ♩♩♩ notes.

3. Play on the piano and sing the finger numbers or words.

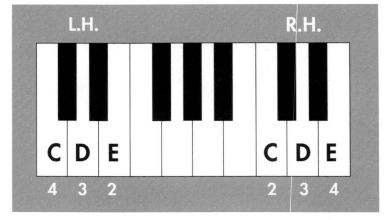

L.H.　　　　　　　　　R.H.

C D E　　　C D E
4 3 2　　　2 3 4

Words by Crystal Bowman

Mon - sieur Mouse,　　Mon - sieur Mouse　　wel - comes friends　　to　his　house.
Plays　gui - tar,　　sings　a　song.　　His　guests dance　　all　night　long.

L.H.
f
C　　D　　E　　E　　D　　C　　D　　D　　D　　E　　E　　E
4　　3　　2　　2　　3　　4　　3　　　　　2

Teacher Duet: (Student plays in the MIDDLE of the keyboard.)

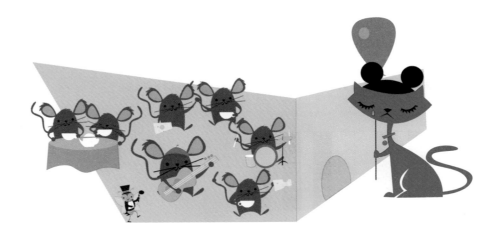

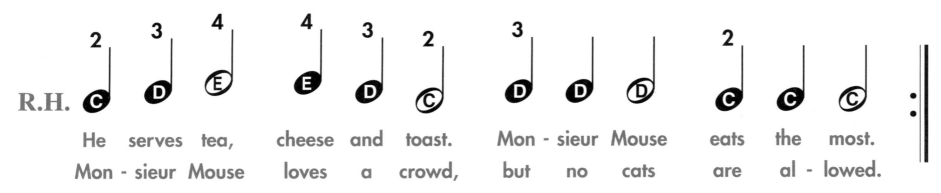

R.H.

2	3	4	4	3	2	3			2		
C	D	E	E	D	C	D	D	D	C	C	C

He serves tea, cheese and toast. Mon - sieur Mouse eats the most.

Mon - sieur Mouse loves a crowd, but no cats are al - lowed.

4. Have fun squeaking the sounds to *Mouse Rhythms*
   in your Writing Book, pp. 32–33.

♩ Can you find Tap?

25

Raccoon's Lullaby

Half-Note Song with Alternating Hands

A lullaby is a song that helps someone go to sleep. Katie is singing to her favorite stuffed animal.

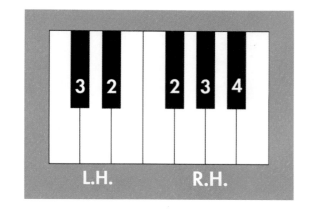

L.H.　　　R.H.

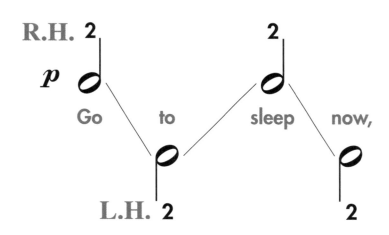

R.H. **2**　　　　　**2**

p

Go　to　sleep　now,　my　rac - coon,　my　rac - coon.

L.H. **2**　　　　　**2**

Teacher Duet: (Student plays HIGHER on the keyboard.)

✎ | WRITING BOOK **34–35 (Animal Riddles and Red Cat, Blue Cat!)**　　　　　　FF1

Tips from Katie: (pp. 50–51)

1. Point to each note, counting, "1-2, 1-2," etc.
   Use **L.H.** for *down*-stems and **R.H.** for *up*-stems.

2. Guide your teacher! Point to each note
   and say the **finger number** as your teacher plays.

3. Play on the piano, singing the finger numbers.
   Have fun singing with the audio!

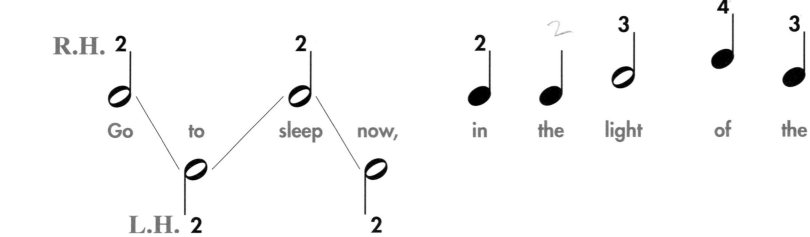

Go   to   sleep   now,   in   the   light   of   the   moon.

Bass Clef

The left hand uses the bass clef for LOW sounds.

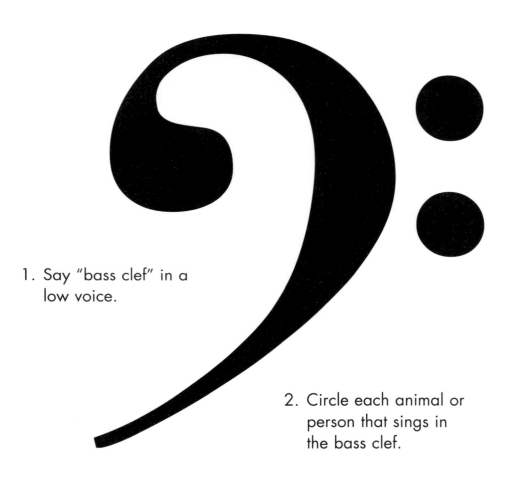

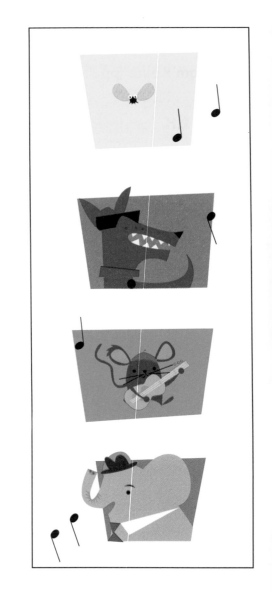

1. Say "bass clef" in a low voice.

2. Circle each animal or person that sings in the bass clef.

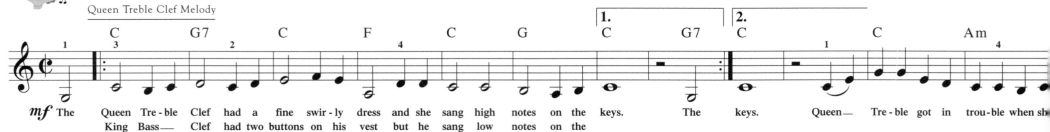

Queen Treble Clef Melody

	C	G7	C	F	C	G	1. C	G7	2. C	C	Am

mf The Queen Tre-ble Clef had a fine swir-ly dress and she sang high notes on the keys. The keys. Queen— Tre-ble got in trou-ble when sh
King Bass— Clef had two buttons on his vest but he sang low notes on the

Treble Clef

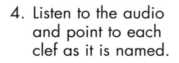

The right hand uses the treble clef for HIGH sounds.

1. Say "treble clef" in a high voice.

2. Circle each animal or person that sings in the treble clef.

3. Your teacher will play a **LOW** or **HIGH** sound. Quickly place R.H. or L.H. on the correct clef.

4. Listen to the audio and point to each clef as it is named.

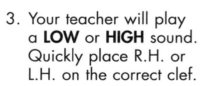

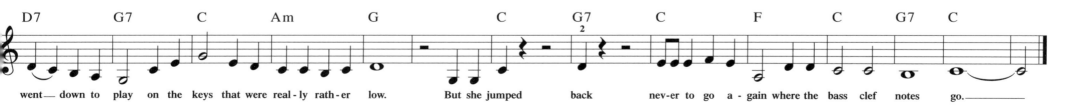

went— down to play on the keys that were real-ly rath-er low. But she jumped back nev-er to go a - gain where the bass clef notes go.———

Mary's Rockin' Pets

(28)

C-D-E Melody with Half Notes

Tips from your friends:

1. As your teacher plays, point to each note and say the **letter name**.

2. Write **f** or **p** for the animal before each verse.

3. Play and sing the finger numbers, letter names, or words.

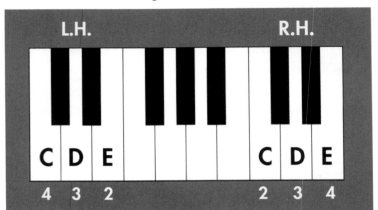

Traditional, words adapted

Mar - y	had	a	lit - tle	lamb,	lit - tle	lamb,	lit - tle	lamb,
Car - los	had	a	lit - tle	horse,	lit - tle	horse,	lit - tle	horse,
Ka - tie	had	a	lit - tle	dog,	lit - tle	dog,	lit - tle	dog,
Dal - las	had	a	lit - tle	chick,	lit - tle	chick,	lit - tle	chick,

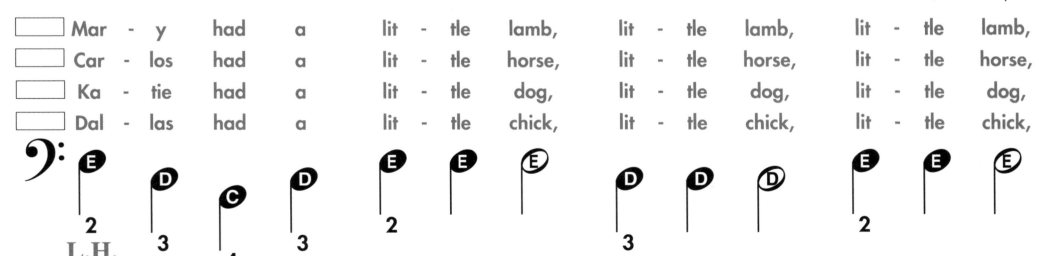

Teacher Duet: (Student plays HIGHER on the keyboard.)

R.H.

	Mar - y	had	a	lit - tle	lamb,	it	was	white	as	snow - flakes.
	Car - los	had	a	lit - tle	horse,	it	was	brown	as	choc - 'late.
	Ka - tie	had	a	lit - tle	dog,	it	was	black	as	mid - night.
	Dal - las	had	a	lit - tle	chick,	it	was	bright	as	sun - shine.

NEW! GRAND STAFF GAMES

Turn to p. 86 and learn about the grand staff.

Teacher Note: These games will prepare students to read on the grand staff.

Whole Note = 4 Beats

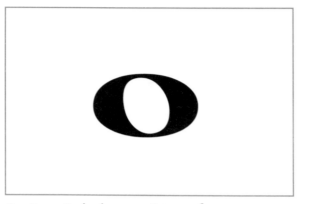

1. Say "whole note" in a **forte** voice,
   piano voice, high voice, low voice.

count: 1 - 2 - 3 - 4   1 - 2 - 3 - 4
whole - note - long - note   whole - note - long - note

2. Tap and count aloud **forte**, then **piano**.
   Hold each note for 4 beats.

3. Draw a whole note in each train car.
   Draw FOUR slashes in each car to show **4 beats**.

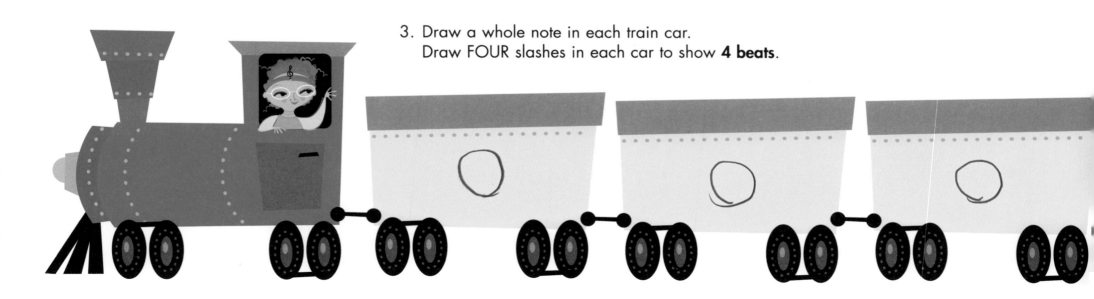

29 Train Rhythms

Tracking the Beat

1. Use a 3-1 donut and play each "train rhythm"
   on **C**, then **D**, then **E.** Count aloud!

2. Your teacher will play a box from each train on **C, D,** or **E.**
   Point to the rhythm you hear and name the key.
   Then you be the teacher!

Which hand plays?

_____

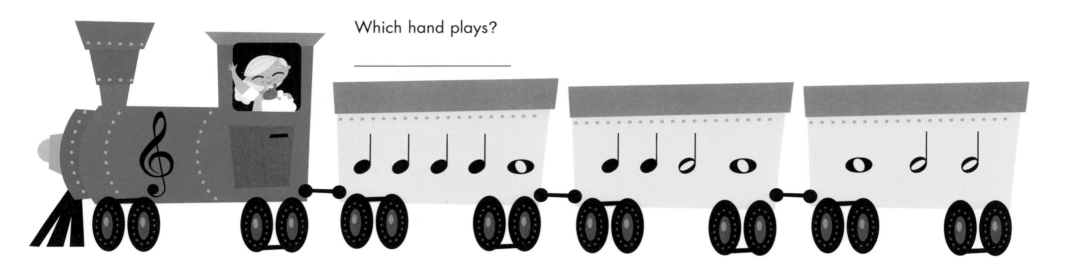

Which hand plays?

_____

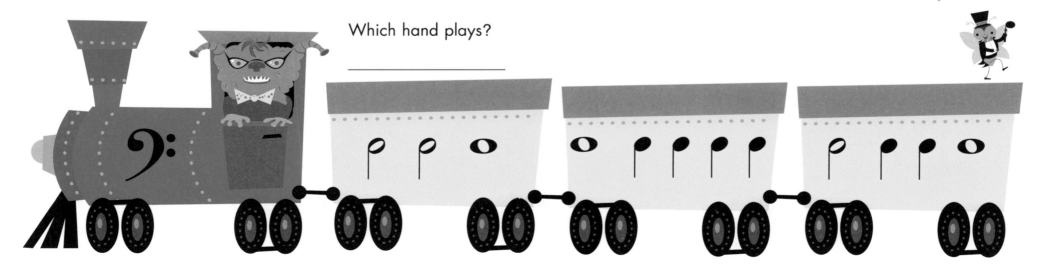

Old Pig-Donald

Black-Key Song with Whole Notes

Old Pig - Don - ald had a song,
Played his key - board all day long,

E - I - E - I - O! (2 - 3 - 4)

repeat

Teacher Duet: (Student plays HIGHER on the keyboard.)

🖉 | WRITING BOOK 42–43 (I Feel Rhythm)   FF

Tips from the farm: (pp. 58–59)

1. Guide your teacher! Point to the notes as your teacher plays the piece.

2. Play on the piano, singing the finger numbers or words.

3. After playing the duet, make up your own farm music. Use only **black keys.**
   When your teacher says, "Return to the farm!" play the first page again.

4. Have fun tapping *I Feel Rhythm* in your Writing Book, pp. 42–43.

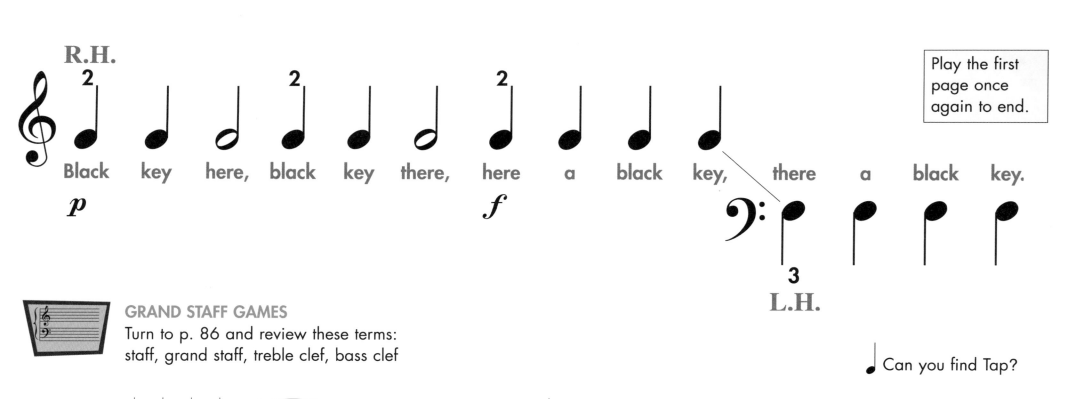

GRAND STAFF GAMES
Turn to p. 86 and review these terms:
staff, grand staff, treble clef, bass clef

3rd.

Shepherd, Count Your Sheep
Black-Key Song with Whole Notes

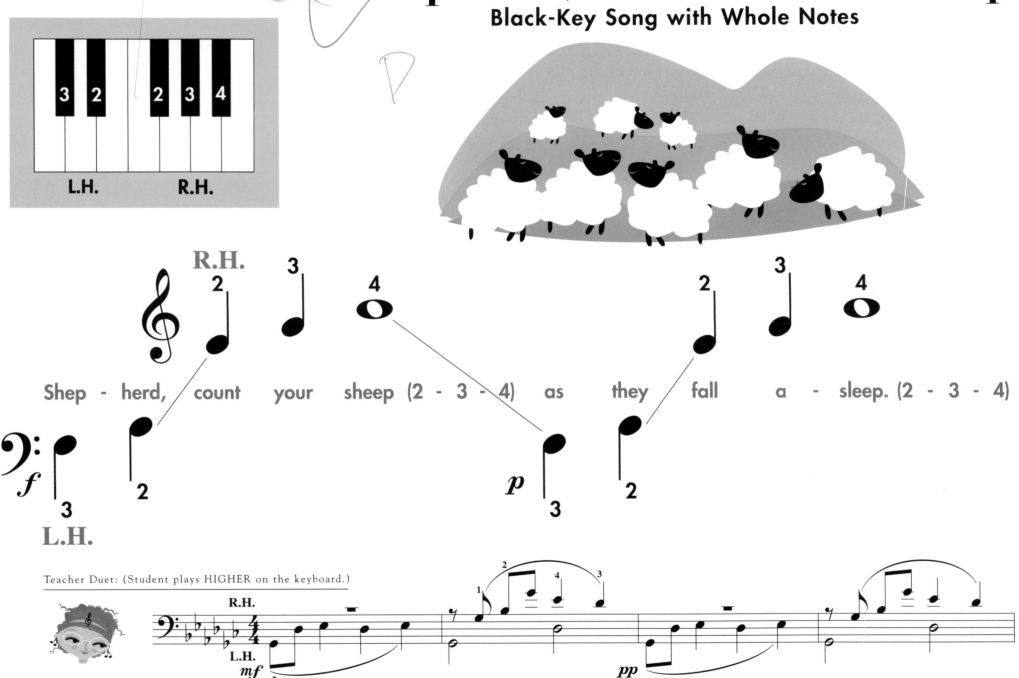

Shep - herd, count your sheep (2 - 3 - 4) as they fall a - sleep. (2 - 3 - 4)

Teacher Duet: (Student plays HIGHER on the keyboard.)

✏️|WRITING BOOK 44–45 (Shepherds, Count Your Beats and Fruity Faces)   F

Tips from Carlos: (pp. 60–61)

1. Point to the notes as your teacher plays.
   Your teacher may ask you to count aloud.

2. Play on the piano and sing the finger numbers or words.
   Your teacher may press the pedal as you play.

3. Make up your own peaceful shepherd music. Play any black keys
   with the teacher duet. End softly on the highest black key.

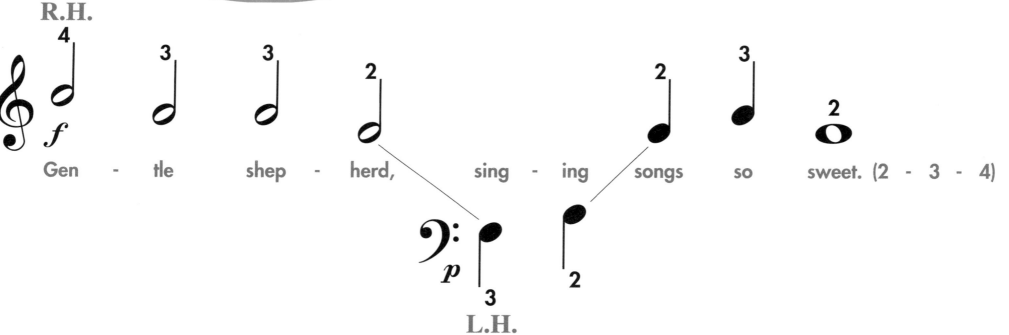

Gen - tle   shep - herd,   sing - ing   songs   so   sweet. (2 - 3 - 4)

The Music Alphabet (33)

Exploring Alphabet Steps

1. Can you say or sing the entire alphabet for your teacher?

The **music alphabet** has only **7** letters.

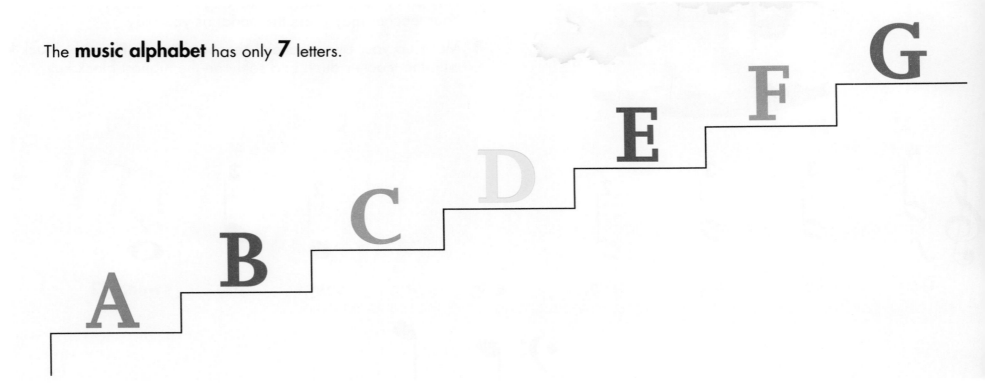

2. Begin with **A**.

   Point to each letter and say it aloud.
   You are STEPPING UP the music alphabet.

3. Begin with **G**.

   Point to each letter and say it aloud.
   You are STEPPING DOWN the music alphabet.
   Sing the alphabet letters with the audio!

Cookie's Journey Up the Mountain

YOUR COOKIE JOURNEY

1. Make a round cookie shape with **L.H. fingers 3 and 1.**
Pretend you are carrying a cookie up a tall mountain (the keyboard).

2. Begin on the lowest key, **A.** Play and say the music alphabet going up the keyboard: **A B C D E F G.**

3. Stop on each **G** so that Dallas can "catch his breath."

4. At the MIDDLE of the keyboard, pass the "3-1 cookie" over to the R.H. Carry the cookie to the top of the piano. Keep saying the music alphabet aloud as you climb.

5. End on **C** for cookie!
Pretend to eat your cookie. What flavor is it?

Technique: C and F across the Keyboard

Tips from Carlos:

1. The *Here Comes the Bride* music must play **7 times** for the baboon bride to reach the groom.

2. After playing this song, try *Rockin' on C and F* with the audio. You and your teacher make up rockin' rhythms on any **C** and **F** keys with the music. Use **finger 3's** as in this song.

The 2-black keys help you find **C**.

The 3-black keys help you find **F**.

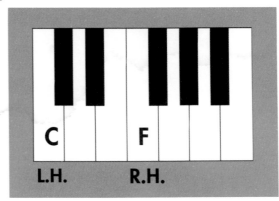

C   F

L.H.   R.H.

36

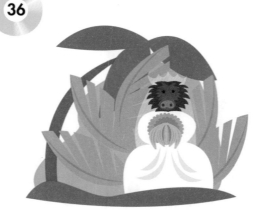

move higher

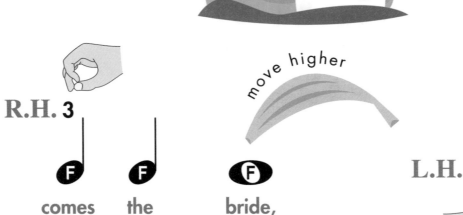

R.H. 3

F   F   F

Here   comes   the   bride,

f

©

L.H.

3

Start on the LOWEST **C** and **F.**

R.H. 3

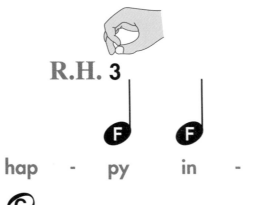

F   F   F

hap - py   in - side!

©

L.H.

3

Move UP the keyboard to the next HIGHER **C** and **F.**

Keep going higher!

    F!

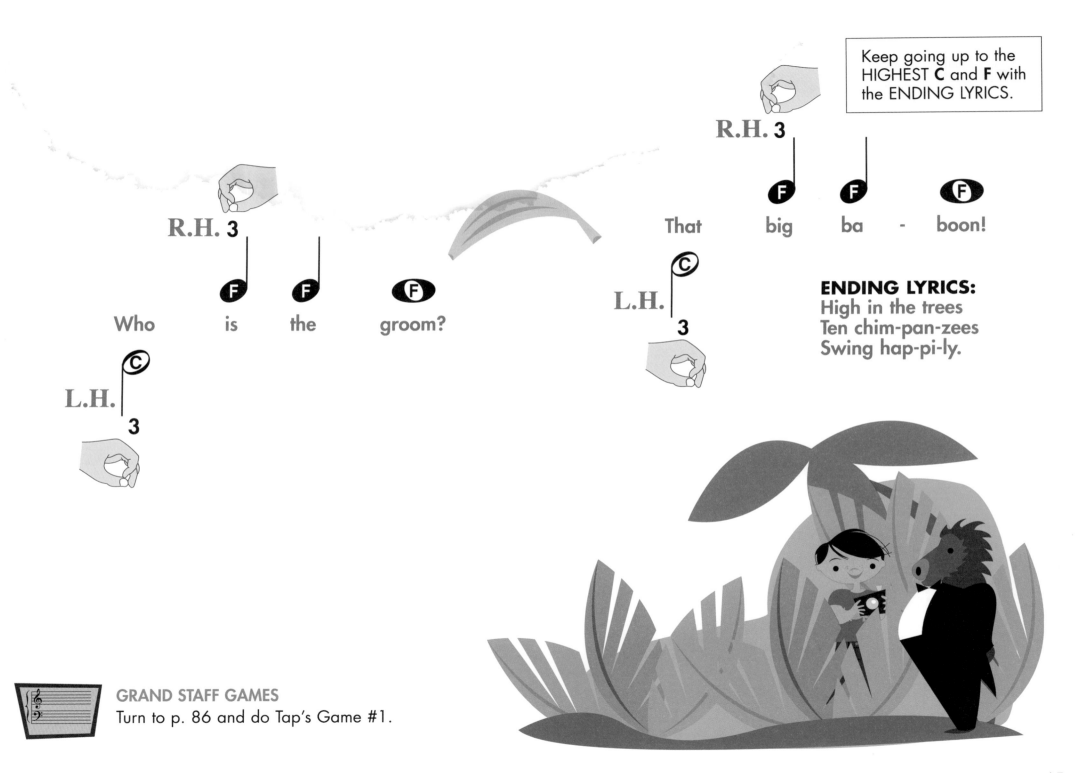

Keep going up to the HIGHEST **C** and **F** with the ENDING LYRICS.

R.H. **3**

F

F

That

F

big ba - boon!

R.H. **3**

F

F

F

Who is the groom?

C

L.H.

3

C

L.H.

3

ENDING LYRICS:
High in the trees
Ten chim-pan-zees
Swing hap-pi-ly.

GRAND STAFF GAMES
Turn to p. 86 and do Tap's Game #1.

Riding the Escalator

Tips from your friends:

1. Pretend a group of friends are riding up the escalator.
   Your teacher will play and demonstrate a smooth ride.
   (Note: The student may move the bench and stand to play.)

2. Have fun crossing the L.H. *over* as the R.H. is playing.
   This will give the friends a smooth ride!

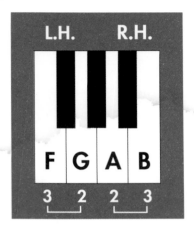

the 4-white keys
just below the
3-black keys

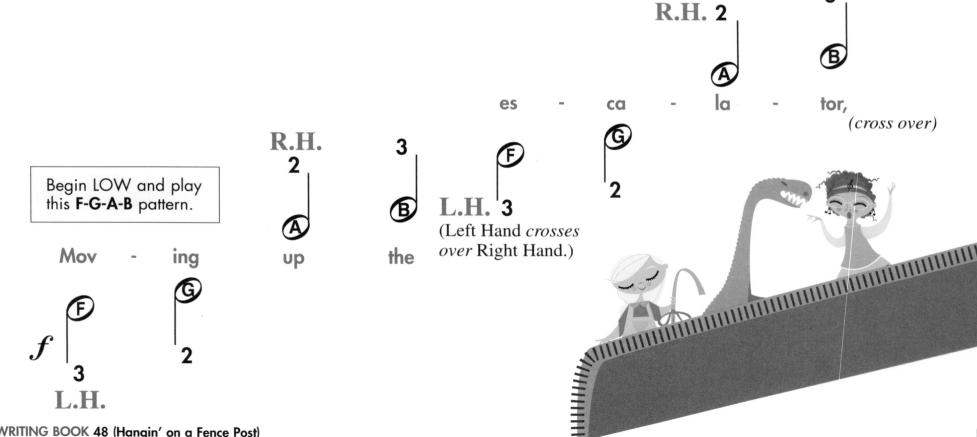

Begin LOW and play
this **F-G-A-B** pattern.

*(Left Hand crosses
over Right Hand.)*

(cross over)

Mov - ing   up   the   es - ca - la - tor,

3. Have fun singing and doing the motions for *Hangin' on a Fence Post*, Writing Book, pp. 48–49. **38**

Sneak-y Thumb

Technique: Playing the Thumb

1. There are four keyboards below. On the piano, "sneak" your **R.H. thumb** up to each key with a red letter. Follow the directions to the right.

2. Repeat with your **L.H. thumb**.

Directions for Sneak-y Thumb

Let your R.H. thumb reach out, with the rest of the fingers "hiding" in a loose fist.

On the piano, sneak the R.H. thumb up to **F** (for example).

Let the other fingers "come out" and rest on the keys. Notice your round hand!

Teacher Duet for *Birthday Train*, p. 69: (Student plays HIGHER on the keyboard.)

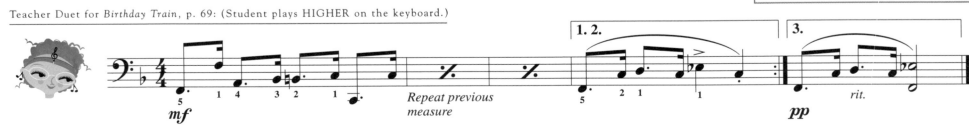

Birthday Train

Song using F-G-A-B

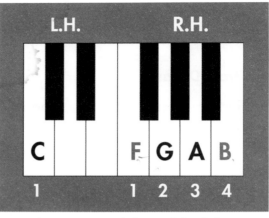

1. Find your new hand position. Hint! Sneak your thumbs up to **C** and **F**.

2. Play and sing finger numbers, letters, or words. Listen for the distant train whistle at the end!

F and **B** surround the **3-black keys.** Play these together for a train whistle!

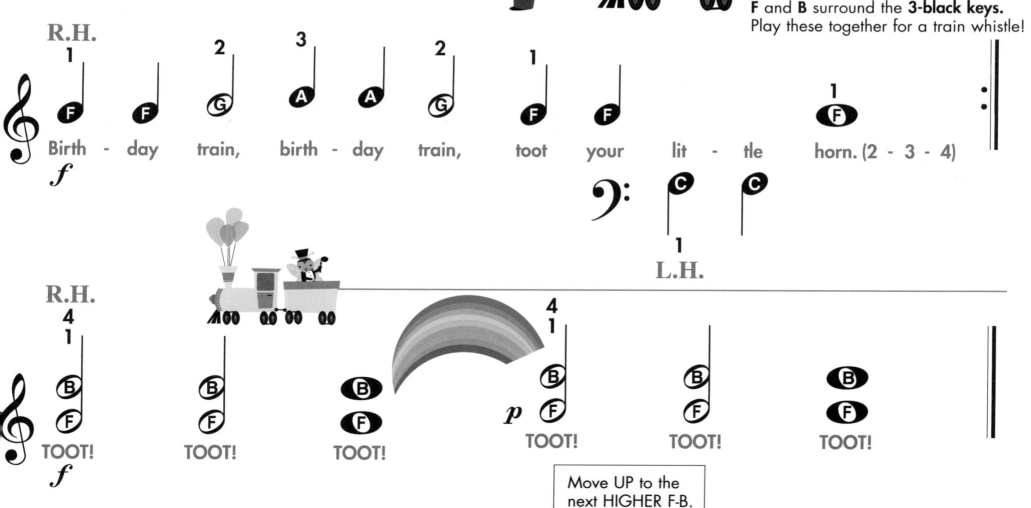

R.H.

Birth - day train, birth - day train, toot your lit - tle horn. (2 - 3 - 4)

f

L.H.

R.H.

TOOT! TOOT! TOOT! *p* TOOT! TOOT! TOOT!

f

Move UP to the next HIGHER F-B.

Wish I Were a Fish

Song using F-G-A-B

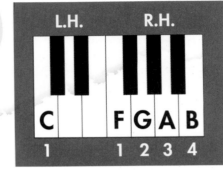

Tips from Dallas:

1. Find your hand position. "Sneak" your thumbs up to **C** and **F**.

2. Play and sing finger numbers, letters, or words.

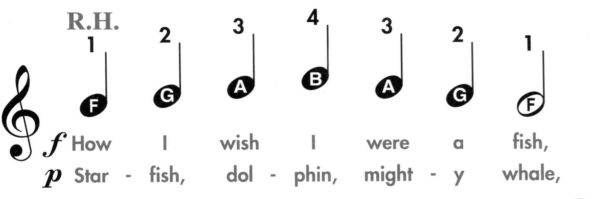

f How   I   wish   I   were   a   fish,   in   the   blue   sea. 2 - 3 - 4

p Star - fish,   dol - phin,   might - y   whale,   so   much   to   see! 2 - 3 - 4

L.H.

Teacher Duet: (Student plays HIGHER on the keyboard.)

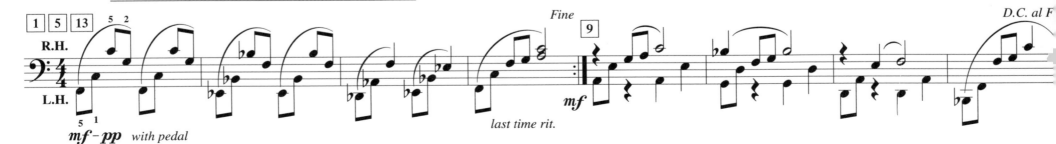

🖉|WRITING BOOK 50–51 (Boa Constrictor)

R.H.
3 — A — Ride
A — a
2 — G — sea - horse,
1 — F — may
2 — G — be
3 — A — two!
play together
3 — A / 1 — F — 2 - 3 - 4

𝆑

𝄢 C / 1 — L.H.

R.H.
1 — F — Wish
2 — G — that
3 — A — I
4 — B — could
3 — A — be
2 — G — a
1 — F — fish,
1 — F — would
1 — F — you
1 — F — be
one   too? 2 - 3 - 4

3. Have fun with key names and play *Boa Constrictor* in the Writing Book, pp. 50–51.

41

𝄢 C / C / 1 — L.H.

Oh! I Love Snack Time

Tips from Carlos and Katie:

1. Point to the notes and say the **letter names** as your teacher plays.

2. Find your hand position. Sing finger numbers and play on your fingertips!

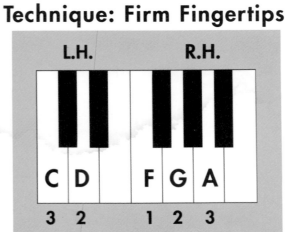

Technique: Firm Fingertips

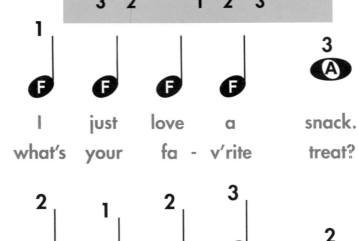

R.H.

3

A A A A

2

G G G

1

F F F F

3

A

f

| When | my | tum | - | my | starts | to | growl, | I | just | love | a | snack. |
| Ranch | dress | - | ing | with | car | - | rot | sticks, | what's | your | fa | - | v'rite | treat? |

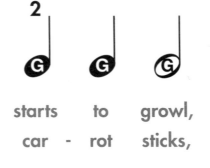

R.H.

1

F

2

G

1

F

2

G

3

A

2

G

| Cheese | and | crisp | - | y | crack | - | ers, | please, | Yum, | my | lips | go | smack! |
| Green | and | pur | - | ple | grapes | are | fun, | rai | - | sins | are | so | sweet. |

D D D D

C C

2

L.H.

3

FF

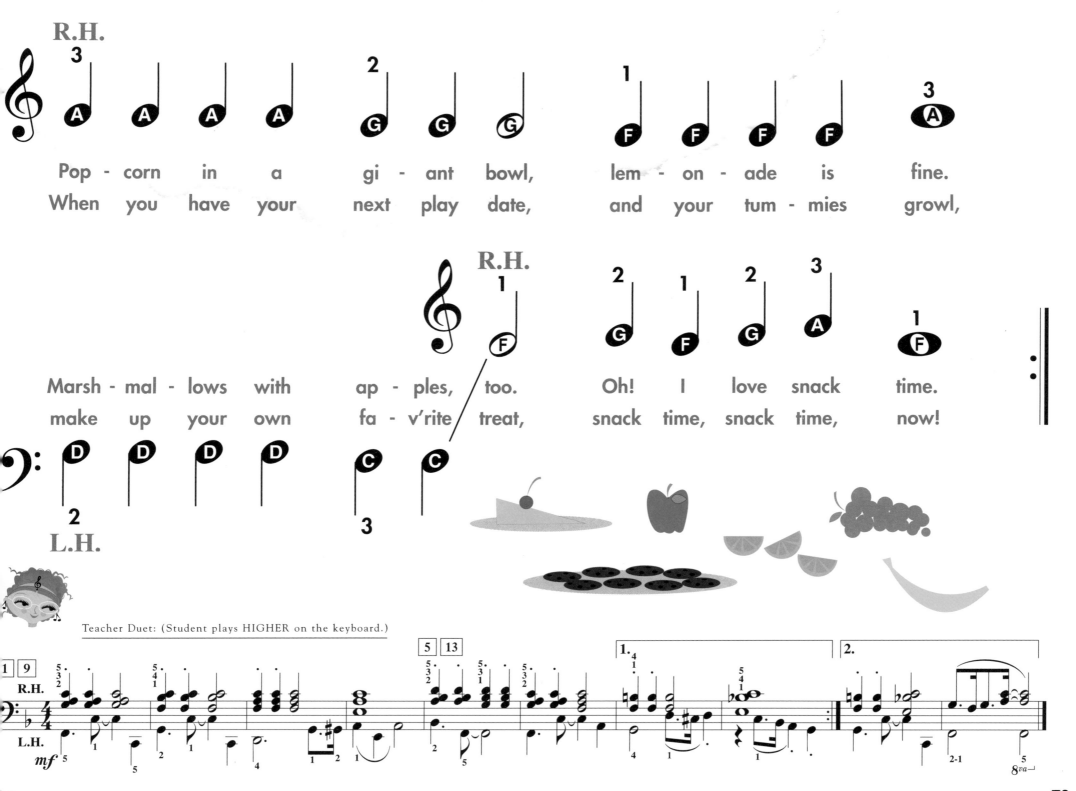

If You're Happy

Key-Name Review

Teacher Directions:

1. Student names each **key with a star** on p. 75.

2. Student practices finding each starred key quickly on the keyboard.

3. Play *If You're Happy* with the teacher part or audio. Student plays each key two times, as in the lyric.*

Teacher Piano Part

VERSE 1

If you're hap-py and you know it, play two C's. (C C) If you're hap-py and you know it, play two F's. (F F) If you're hap-py and you know it and you real-ly want to show it, if you're

hap-py and you know it, play two D's. (D D) If you're hap-py and you know it, play two E's. (E E) If you're hap-py and you know it, play two D's. (D D) If you're

VERSE 2

hap-py and you know it, and you real-ly want to show it, if you're hap-py and you know it, play two D's. (D D) If you're hap-py and you know it, play two G's. (G G) If you're

VERSE 3

hap-py and you know it, play two B's. (B B) If you're hap-py and you know it, and you real-ly want to show it, find two A's. Play them for-te on the keys! (A A)

*★★ = student

74

FF

Student Part

Verse 1:

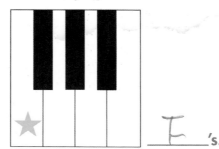

If you're happy and you
know it, play TWO

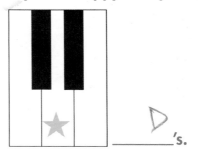

If you're happy and you
know it, play TWO

If you're happy and you know it,
and you really want to show it,
If you're happy and you know it, play TWO

C 's.

E 's.

D 's.

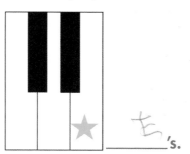

Verse 2:

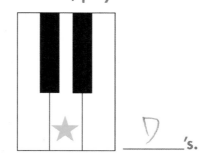

If you're happy and you
know it, play TWO

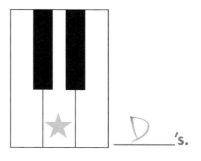

If you're happy and you
know it, play TWO

If you're happy and you know it,
and you really want to show it,
If you're happy and you know it, play TWO

E 's.

D 's.

D 's.

Verse 3:

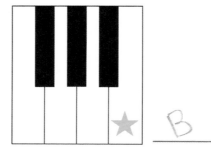

If you're happy and you
know it, play TWO

If you're happy and you
know it, play TWO

If you're happy and you know it,
and you really want to show it,
find TWO A's. Play them *forte* on the keys.

G 's.

B 's.

A 's.

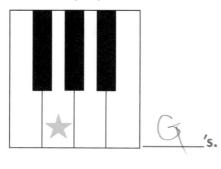

My L.H. C Scale

Playing L.H. Fingers 5-4-3-2-1

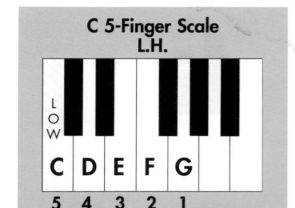

**C 5-Finger Scale
L.H.**

LOW

C D E F G

5 4 3 2 1

In music, a scale is like a ladder that steps
UP or DOWN from one key to the next.

Begin on a
LOWER C.

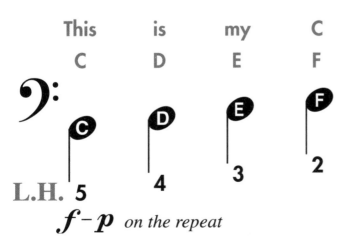

| This | is | my | C | scale. (2 - 3 - 4) | This | is | my | C | scale. (2 - 3 - 4) |
| C | D | E | F | G (2 - 3 - 4) | G | F | E | D | C (2 - 3 - 4) |

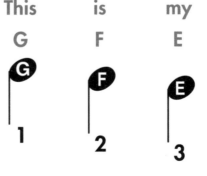

L.H. 5   4   3   2   1   1   2   3   4   5

f - *p* *on the repeat*

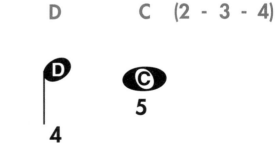

GRAND STAFF GAMES
Turn to p. 87 and do Tap's Game #2.

Tips from Mrs. Razzle-Dazzle: (pp. 76–77)

1. Do *Stone on the Mountain* with each hand as a warm-up (pp. 12–13).

2. On the closed keyboard cover, play and say the **finger numbers** for both hands.

3. Find the **C 5-finger scale** on the piano for each hand. Sing letter names or the words. Can you see your "stone"?

CDEFG

My R.H. C Scale
Playing R.H. Fingers 1-2-3-4-5

C 5-Finger Scale
R.H.

Begin on MIDDLE C.

R.H.

1	2	3	4	5	5	4	3	2	1
C	D	E	F	G	G	F	E	D	C

This is my C scale. (2 - 3 - 4) This is my C scale. (2 - 3 - 4)

C D E F G (2 - 3 - 4) G F E D C (2 - 3 - 4)

f-p *on the repeat*

Teacher Duet: (Student plays HIGHER on the keyboard.) Use for pp. 76 and 77.

R.H.

L.H.

mp-pp on repeat

The Measure

Grouping Beats

In music, the notes are grouped into **measures**.
Think of a measure as a musical room.

Each measure has the same number of counts (beats).
Bar lines divide the music into measures.

Think of bar lines as the walls of the music room.

bar line　　　　　　　　　　　　**bar line**

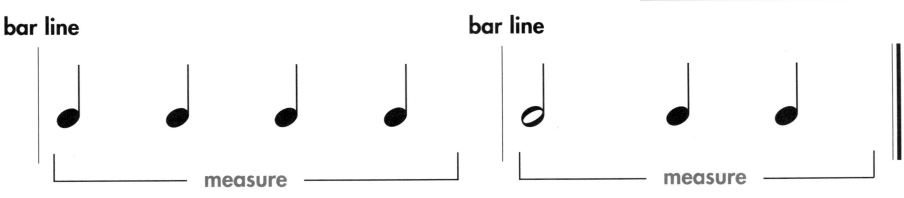

measure　　　　　　　　　　　　measure

Review:
Double Bar Line means the end.

one **thin** line
one **thick** line

Tips from Carlos :

1. Can you circle each **bar line** above?

2. How many beats are in each measure above? Circle a number in this blue box.

3. Turn to *Monsieur Mouse* on p. 48. Can you draw bar lines after every **4 beats**?

1　2　3　4

Katie's Dog Tuck

C 5-Finger Scale Song

Tips from Tucker:

1. Guide your teacher! Point to each note and say the **letter names** as your teacher plays.

2. Place your hands in the **C 5-finger scale**. Play, singing finger numbers, letter names, or words.

Words by Crystal Bowman

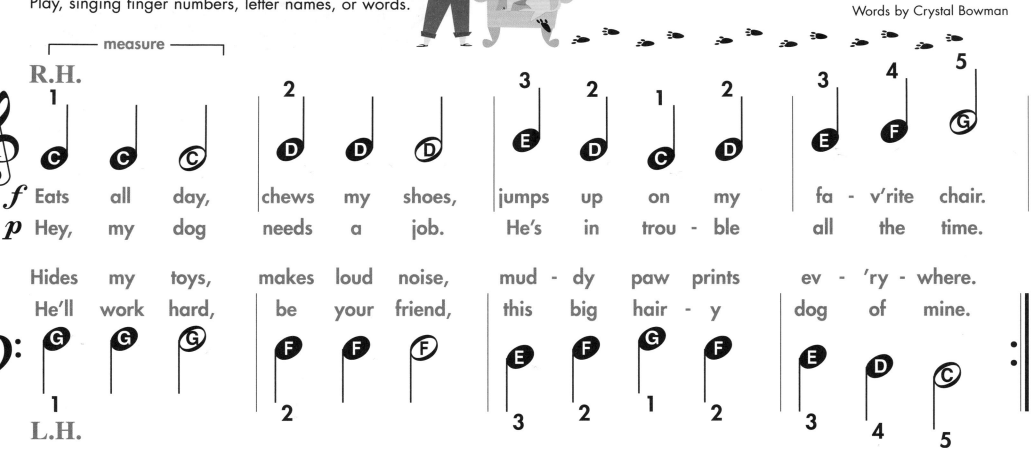

f Eats	all	day,	chews	my	shoes,	jumps	up	on	my	fa -	v'rite	chair.
p Hey,	my	dog	needs	a	job.	He's	in	trou -	ble	all	the	time.
Hides	my	toys,	makes	loud	noise,	mud - dy	paw	prints	ev - 'ry - where.
He'll	work	hard,	be	your	friend,	this	big	hair - y	dog	of	mine.

Teacher Duet: (Student plays HIGHER on the keyboard.)

Play two times, 2nd time *p*.

✎ WRITING BOOK 55 (I Look in the Mirror)

Bed on a Boat
C 5-Finger Scale Song

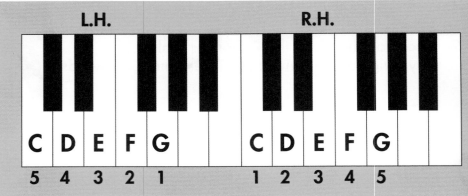

Words by Crystal Bowman

Tips from Carlos:

1. Listen to your teacher play just the duet. Sway gently back and forth, as if you are rocking on a boat.

2. Guide your teacher! Point to each note saying the **letter name** as she/he plays the piece.

3. Play singing finger numbers, letter names, or words.

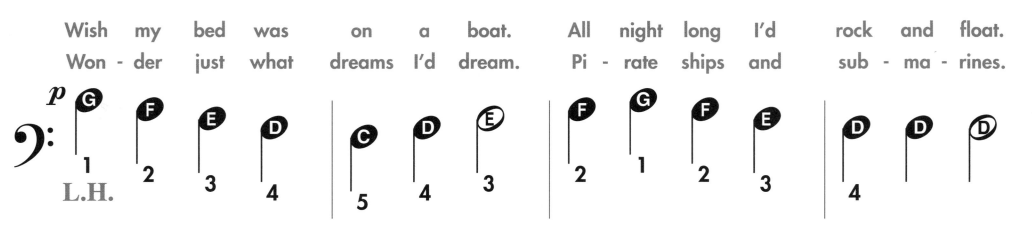

Wish my bed was on a boat. All night long I'd rock and float.
Won - der just what dreams I'd dream. Pi - rate ships and sub - ma - rines.

Teacher Duet: (Student plays HIGHER on the keyboard.)

✏️|WRITING BOOK 56–57 (I Hear Thunder!)

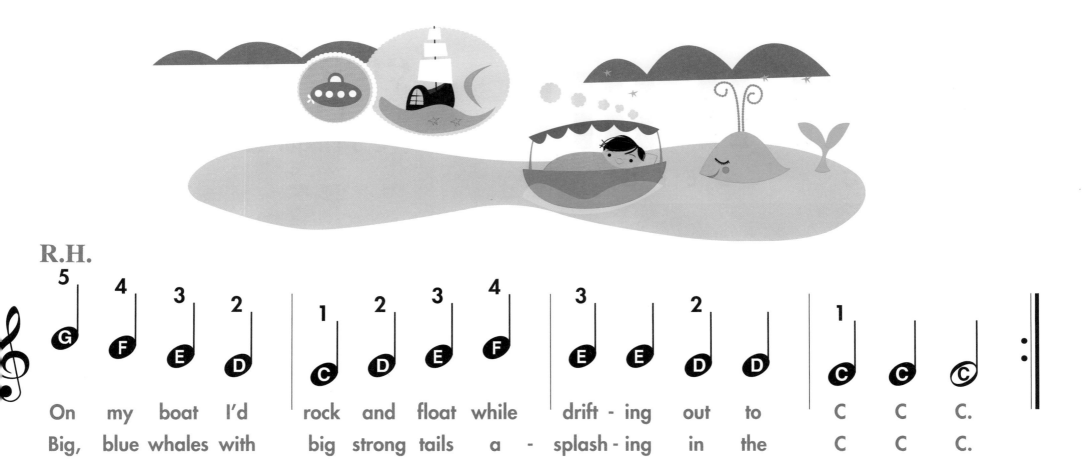

R.H.

5	4	3	2		1	2	3	4		3	2		1		
G	F	E	D		C	D	E	F		E E	D	D		C C C	

On   my   boat   I'd | rock   and   float while | drift - ing   out   to | C   C   C.
Big, blue whales with | big   strong tails   a   - | splash - ing   in   the | C   C   C.

 GRAND STAFF GAMES
Turn to p. 87 and do Tap's Game #3.

Use Tucker's Tips from p. 79.

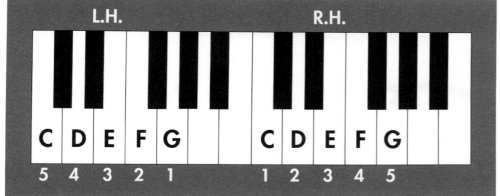

Eensie Weensie Spider

47

C 5-Finger Scale Song

R.H.

Een - sie Ween - sie | Spi - der climbed on Mid - dle | C. (2 - 3 - 4)

f

Down came my hands, she jumped right down to E! (2 - 3 - 4)

L.H.

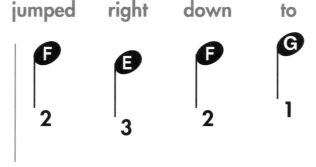

Teacher Duet: (Student plays VERY HIGH on the keyboard.)

Play 3 times.

R.H.

L.H.

mp

✐ |WRITING BOOK 58–59 (A Lesson from Eensie Weensie Spider's Momma)

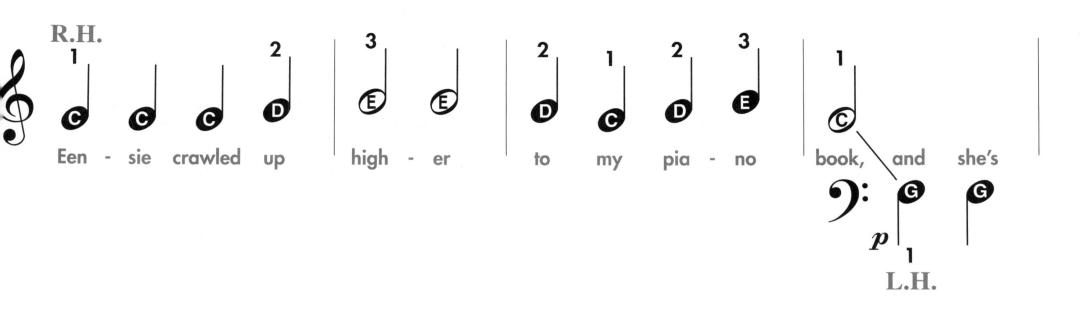

R.H.

Een - sie crawled up | high - er | to my pia - no | book, and she's

L.H.

p

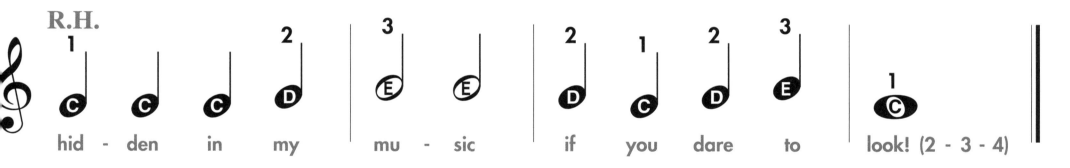

R.H.

hid - den in my | mu - sic | if you dare to | look! (2 - 3 - 4)

GRAND STAFF GAMES

Turn to pp. 86-87 and review Tap's Game #1, #2, and #3.

♩ Can you find the musical spider?

13

pp

f

48

Graduation Party

C 5-Finger Scale Melody

Tips from your friends:

1. Guide your teacher! Point to each note and say the **letter name** as your teacher plays.

2. On the closed keyboard, play the song and say finger numbers.

3. Place your hands in the **C 5-finger scale**. Play and sing finger numbers, letter names, or words.

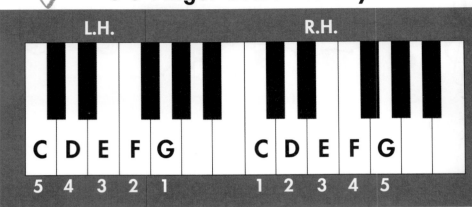

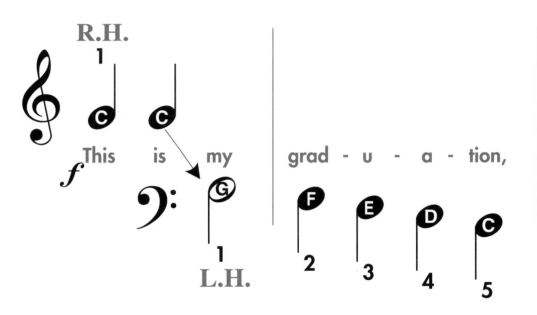

R.H.

This   is   my   grad - u - a - tion,   Book   A   grad - u - a - tion   par - ty,

L.H.

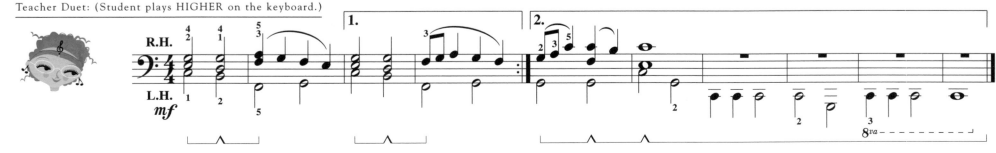

Teacher Duet: (Student plays HIGHER on the keyboard.)

✎ |WRITING BOOK 60–61 (C Scale Animal Parade and Carlos Says, "Play C-D-E-F-G")

Grand Staff Games

Piano music uses two staffs.

A staff has **5 lines** and **4 spaces**.

Together we call them the **GRAND STAFF.**

Tap's Game #1

Learn the word STAFF.

Count the **5 lines** and **4 spaces.**

Your teacher will point to a line. Can you name the number?

Your teacher will point to any note. Say "line" or "space" for that note.

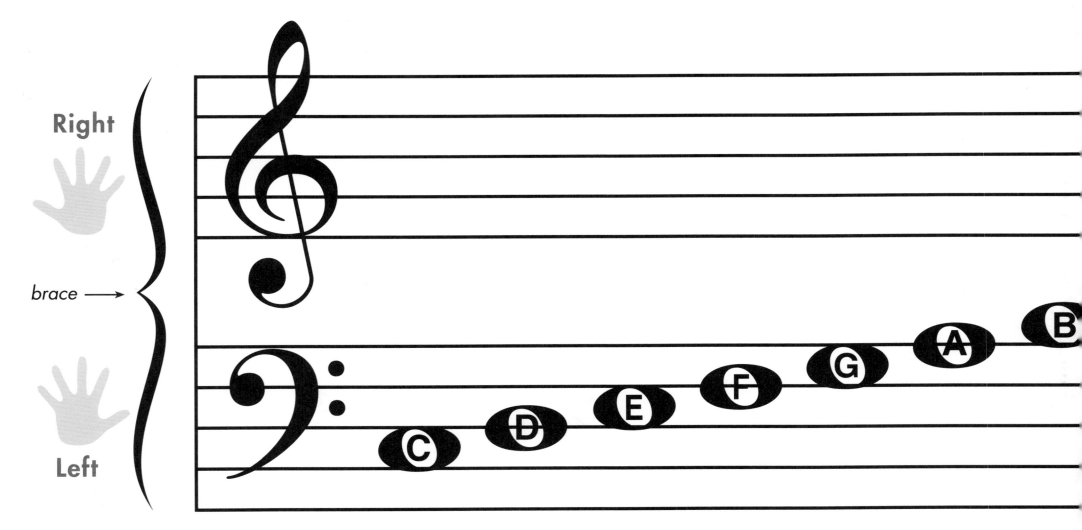

Right

Left

brace →

Tap's Game #2

Say the word GRAND STAFF.

Find and name the **treble** and **bass clef.**

Your teacher will play HIGH or LOW notes. Point to the 𝄞 with your **R.H.** or the 𝄢 with your **L.H.** for the sound.

Tap's Game #3

Point to each SPACE note and name it.
Begin on the LOW C and move to the right.
Notice you are skipping the line notes.

Point to each LINE note and name it.
Begin on the LOW D and move to the right.
Notice you are skipping the space notes.

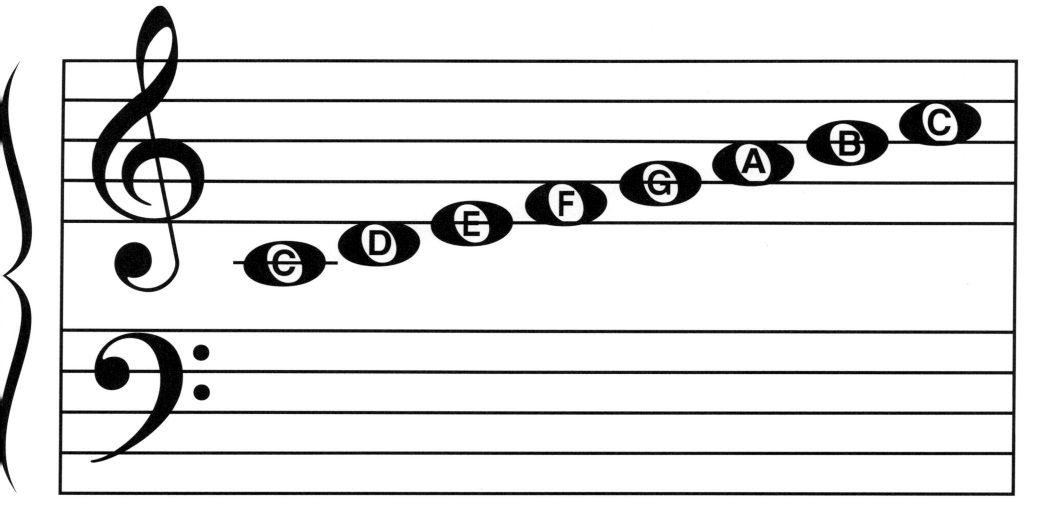

Certificate for Lesson Book A

_____

(Sign and join the club!)

We can't wait to see you in Lesson Book B!